More Enlightened Than A Jacket Potato

Jack Prefontaine

About the Author

Jack Prefontaine has helped hundreds of people heal and develop spiritually after a traumatic incident in his early 20s left him off work with PTSD for ten months and on a search for "spiritual enlightenment", which he epically failed at. Jack combines insight from High Performance Sport, his Psychology MSc and extensive spiritual training to help people live a life of radiant peace- full of vibrant health, loving relationships and career success.

www.jackprefontaine.com

Contents

Introduction: Be careful what you wish for

Introduction-
Be careful what you wish for

There was a knock on my flat. I wasn't expecting any deliverers or any friends to visit, so I was intrigued about who was there. The intrigue built further when I opened the door. Stood in front of me was a tall man just over six foot, with bulging muscles, slick black hair, cigarette in hand, tattoos all over his body and a look in his eye that made you know he was not a bloke to be messed with. In contrast I was a weedy University student. Living on my own on the edge of Exeter, whilst studying in my 3rd year at the university, I was a High Performance Sports Coach by day to my peers and by night a dedicated searcher for the ultimate spiritual truth of enlightenment. It had all started after a profound experience aged twenty in my second year at University. Since then I had repeatedly prayed for God to bring me a spiritual messenger to show me the way to enlightenment, having got tired of reading all my spiritual books and meditating for hours on end each day. Be careful what you wish for.

Unsure and scared of exactly what this beast of a man wanted with me, I was relieved to find out that he only wanted my support with a noise complaint of a neighbour upstairs in our block of nine flats. Oh yes the neighbour upstairs. The weed addict who constantly went crazy by seemingly smashing things against the wall and verbally abusing his girlfriend, making it very difficult to sometimes get sleep at night. I weighed things up in my mind. Would I rather potentially piss off the weed addict (who was quite a small and thin man) or upset this beast of a man in front of me by not supporting his noise complaint? The beast of the man won.

Then something extraordinary happened.

'Are you spiritual?' questioned the man after we had both had a good moan about the weed addict and I agreed to support him in his noise complaint. This caught me off guard.

'Erm yes I am I suppose,' I replied, very unsure about what exactly he meant by spiritual. I wouldn't have expected a

1

spiritual person to have tattoos, be smoking a cigarette and look like he should be in some sort of mafia film. So I played it careful.

'I saw you with a buddhist book the other day mate,' he explained. 'You the religious type or more spiritual?'

'Definitely spiritual and not religious,' I confirmed, starting to relax into the conversation with this strange guy. 'I was just looking into Buddhism to see what it could help me with on my spiritual path but I don't believe in religion at all to be honest.'

'That's my lad,' he exclaimed, clenching his tattooed fist together and offering to give me a fist pump. I bumped fists with him. 'Hey man let me read your aura for you. I've been doing loads of training on it recently and I need to try it out on some people'

This was just getting freaking now. How did this random dude know about auras? Holy fuck I thought…maybe he actually is spiritual. We were still standing outside my front door on the bottom floor of the flats at this point and I was just about to invite him into my flat but he was already fully flowing with reading my aura.

'A lot of anger in the heart. I feel suppression and emotional wounds from the mother. There is also a suppression in the sacral chakra- doesn't feel like your getting a lot of pussy. Root chakra is ok- your quite grounded in your own way. Throat chakra is nice and open- you like talking right? Ohhh no wow; your top chakra is very open to the heavens- I see a powerful spiritual teacher emerging in you one day.'

He paused for a moment, almost seeking some sort of clarification on something that had interrupted his flow. He did seem to be picking up some accurate things in his own unique way. He suddenly jolted in his body, as some sort of energy moved through him and he moved his head to look me directly in the eye.

'Right your coming with me,' he instructed, pointing towards the exit from the flats. 'We need to take a walk around the Quey and I will help you face your greatest fear'.

Although this was certainly up there with the most bizarre things that had ever happened to me, I felt this sort of trust towards him. There was also excitement. I had been waiting for something interesting to come into my life to help me on my spiritual journey and although this wasn't exactly how I had planned it, I was happy to go with the flow.

I walked out of the door with my new friend, as we walked a couple of streets to the nearby Quey that was its usual hub of tourist activity on this warm summer's day. My new friend suddenly realised he hadn't introduced himself properly.

'I'm Jason by the way. Work in the local B&Q and been on the spiritual path for a number of years now mate,' he shared, putting out his hand for a more formal handshake this time. It did seem all a little late now he was my guide to face my greatest fear. After we had shaken hands we paused for a moment. We both took in the views of the sun beaming down magnificently on the water of the Quey alongside all the people enjoying their lunch eating out and many children tucking into well-deserved ice creams after long walks.

'Right lets get going matey,' instructed Jason, as we started walking again at a much faster pace again. I stayed silent. There was still something in me that trusted this very interesting guy and it made sense that we were getting away from the more busy aspects of the Quey. We continued walking for at least twenty minutes. Eventually we stopped at a point where there were no people, right at the far end of the Quey and away from the main centre of the shops and ice cream vans.

'I want you to look over the edge and into the water,' he instructed. I mean this was getting a little weird now. Checking that he was keeping his distance and wasn't going to throw me to my death from the near twenty-foot drop to the Quey, I composed myself, breathed deeply and looked over.

'I want to imagine yourself falling into the river,' he instructed, still keeping a good distance (maybe a little extra than normal) to re-assure me the falling was all in my mind and not about to happen in the physical. I tried my best to play along. I imagined my body falling into the river, unable to move and then eventually drowning to my death. I had read about these extreme spiritual exercises in Buddhist books. They were designed to reduce the fear of the death of the ego and help you transcend the limitations of human consciousness…in theory anyway. If I was being honest I was struggling and not really feeling anything inside bar a little bit of an idiot for doing this weird exercise with a man in his mid-40s, who I barely knew.

We kept going for what felt like eternity but apparently was only ten minutes according to Jason's re-collection later. I hadn't felt much but tried my best to make out I had encountered some profound spiritual realisations through Jason's crazy exercise. We competed our lap of the Quey, as Jason shared a little more about himself and confirmed that it was a Buddhist Tantric exercise he had asked me to do. I listened intently and as we approached our block invited Jason into my flat for a refreshing drink.

'Do you not have a beer mate?' he enquired, as I offered him a choice of tap water or orange juice. You see at this point I was eating a fully strict fruitarian diet, so wasn't exactly the best host when it came to my choice of food and drink.

'No sorry mate- not aligned with my spiritual diet,' I replied rather arrogantly, with a perplexed and superior look on my face. How could beer be considered part of a spiritual diet?

'Full of spiritual arrogance,' he commented, laughing to himself as he did so and lighting a cigarette. In my house!! I was about to reprimand him for daring to smoke in my flat but then hastily remembered he was more than capable of beating the shit out of me, so I stopped myself.

'One day you will realise real spirituality is about facing your fears and finding peace within, rather than how pathetically spiritual you look on the outside,' he shared, laughing again to himself about my supposed spiritual immaturity. 'Let me show you something to make even as someone as spiritual as you shit themselves,' he instructed, as he adjusted his chair so he was only one metre away from me.

He instructed me to look into his eyes and do my best not to blink. Was he about to reveal himself as an avatar? I had read in an autobiography of a yogi that sometimes the highest spiritual people of the Earth took on a more human form and then revealed themselves once their person for their divine message had relaxed. No that couldn't be it I concluded after 5 seconds of nervously shifting around in my seat. He still very much looked like Jason. The slick mafia style hair was still there, the bulging muscles were still there and so were all the tattoos. Maybe he was about to deliver Darshan to me? I had heard this was an ancient Indian technique where spiritual masters looked into your eyes so you could connect to the peace within.

'For fuck sake, will you just sit still and look into my eyes you nervous prick,' he commented in a tone mixed of aggression and humour. It was enough to make me stop moving around but not enough to hurt my feelings in anyway.

'That's it there we go, try not to blink,' he reminded me, as we looked deeply into each other's eyes.

I had always imagined a moment like this would be reserved for the first love of my life rather than a man in his mid-40s who was trying to teach me things about the spiritual path. Anyway I persisted. Nothing happened for a while but then we started to go deeper. His face became less visible until it completely morphed into the face of an old man, which freaked me out. I kept composed though. His face then changed to that of my mother, before morphing into some sort of alien looking creature. What was happening?

Eventually the fear became too much and I had to pull away.

'Well done,' he commented with a smug smile all across his face. 'You have just seen beyond doubt that your body's eyes lie to you and there are many layers of reality that we are constantly unaware of.'

'What just happened?' I questioned in a stunned tone. 'Did you perform some sort of spiritual magic on me or something?'

'Of course not, you idiot,' he replied, with the smile still beaming across his chiselled face. 'It helps that you are quite spiritually open but you can do it with anyone. The eyes are the windows to the soul as they say,"

After many more questions and some lighter discussion we said our goodbyes. There would be many more conversations and evenings spent with this most mysterious of spiritual messengers. About a week later at the ripe old age of twenty one Jason introduced me to my first proper spiritual teacher (who was part of a mystery school) and also the book A Course In Miracles, which both massively accelerated my spiritual journey beyond all proportion. Be careful what you wish for as they say.

Chapter 1-
Enlightenment experience aged 20

The intense search for enlightenment had started a few years before. After much pain and difficulty with illness in my teenage years I entered University probably unlike any other student in the history of education. My sole purpose was not to party, get a degree or shag loads of hot girls but to find the ultimate answer to life. I had promised myself aged eighteen when I was off school for months with chronic fatigue that I would do everything it took to overcome death and find the ultimate peace. This had led to much searching. I had read book after book on personal growth, a wide range of spiritual books and also started to relentlessly self-enquire into what was happening in my own mind.

I had also made other important shifts by the time I got to University. I was eating only fruit, was only drinking water and was also certainly not engaging in any sexual activity (more on this in the sex chapter). So in short I was one fucking weirdo. Yet I was also someone who was absolutely ready for an authentic direct enlightenment experience, as I was looking after myself in an extremely 'pure' way that meant any profound experiences would only come about at the grace of silence. So much to admire for the spiritual purists and hermits amongst you! I do feel this is an important point though, as so many people think they have an enlightenment experience after taking a drug, doing an ayahuasca 'retreat', getting a healing, seeing a guru/master or in deep meditation. I renounce all those methods for an enlightenment experience. They are certainly full of experiences that could be classed as spiritual and alter your way of life profoundly but direct enlightenment experiences only come at Grace. They are also accompanied by crazy events in your life, which will help you discover very naturally what the hell is going on.

The direct enlightenment experience happened aged twenty in the most unlikely place- right on a fucking hockey pitch at 10pm one night after I had been coaching. This is rare. By saying it is 'rare' I am just being fundamentally honest. You will see throughout this book my very human flaws and limitations laid out to bare, as well as how keen I am to empower you towards your own inner authority (especially spiritual authority). Let me give a little context before I share what exactly happened on that fateful mid-November evening.

I was in my second year studying Sports & Exercise Science at the University of Exeter. I was also in an unusual position. Not only because of my lifestyle but also the position I found myself in as a Sports Coaching Scholar, coaching the Men's 1st XI hockey (the second biggest university sport in England) at the top level of university sport. This had come about in a quite miraculous way. After trying to play hockey in my first year but having to stop a couple of months into the season because of the re-emergence of my chronic fatigue, I had decided to focus on my coaching with a local club and had also been offered the opportunity to do the Men's 1st XI video analysis. The chances of me being offered the opportunity to coach the Men's 1st XI the following season were about a billion to one at this stage- they were one of the top 3 university teams in the UK, full of junior internationals and some senior internationals and also playing one below the top adult league in the country. Half the team were also older than me. Yet when the universe really wants to wake you up it will move mountains to make things happen and through a serious of extraordinary events I found myself coaching the Mens 1st XI the following year, alongside the Director of Hockey who oversaw both the men's and the ladies teams at the university. This really was unprecedented in the hockey world and just made no sense on a rational level, given my experience and age.

By mid-November I was fully in the flow of the challenge of stepping up to this coaching level so young. I wasn't thriving and nor was the team. Having lost fourteen 1st XI players from the year before, we were in a re-building year and were in a relegation battle for the first time in many years. The pressure was building. In many ways the conditions were set perfectly for an enlightenment experience as alongside my lifestyle I was now regularly facing my biggest fear (coaching my peers who I had admired as Gods the year before). I had the solitude of the relatively isolated university life I was living outside of hockey but also the mirror of relationships to go much deeper with the relentless self-enquiry that was now a regular part of my life. The result of facing my biggest fear wasn't pretty. Although when I coached a mysterious force seemed to take over to make me ok, away from the hockey pitch I was suffering from anxiety, depression, deep seated feelings of not being good enough, a fear of being betrayed by the lads and high level of self-hatred that made me always think I was doing something wrong. It was an extreme situation.

On that mid-November evening it was around 9:45pm at night. I had finished coaching and my inner world was full of the normal doubts, self-hatred and feelings I had done something wrong that normally came in full force right after the buzz of the session had ended. I had just cleared the kit away and was about to leave the pitch. At this point it was only me still present on the pitch, as the players had long gone, the Director of Hockey always left at the start of the session after his initial pep talk and there were no other students up at the sports park this late. The hockey pitch was set in a position that made you think you were almost at the top of a holy mountain. It was right at the top of the hilly Exeter Campus and the bright floodlights beaming onto the green astro pitch gave it a poignant mystical feel, like magic was in the air. The silence of the night also helped. It was a normal just above zero degrees English winter evening and pitch black outside of the lit up hockey pitch, with the cold and the darkness also giving the whole setting an otherworldly feel to it. I always felt it was easier to connect to the soul in places like this. For some reason rather than just pack up and leave the pitch, I decided to pause for a moment. I was close to breaking point and very much looking forward to the Xmas break from university and particularly hockey. I hated my life. It was like a never ending box of being stuck in the powerful emotions and depressive thoughts that were out of my control and kept coming up in and around the hockey. I just wanted a break. I just wanted to feel happy. And most of all I just wanted the peace I had read about in all those spiritual books.

'Please help me, I just want to find peace,' I said into the wilderness of the hockey pitch, to no person but hoping spirit may just intervene. 'This is getting too much now, I am at breaking point,' I shared with the silence, tears starting to roll down my eyes as my heart opened and the pain came through in full blast. Nothing happened for the next five seconds, as I looked down into the astro-turf pitch and continued to cry.

Then suddenly out of nowhere it was like my whole inner being exploded. Energy rippled up through my spine and through all areas of my head, as my entire being became totally silenced and I become the silence who could see the complete fickleness of my personality and the attachment to believing my personality that was causing all the suffering. It was like I was suspended in time. All thought had evaporated, all heaviness had left the body, emotions were there but couldn't touch the peace and the sense of separation broke down entirely to reveal peace. The silence wasn't me, it just was. I have no idea how long I spent in awe on that pitch but it was like time had completely collapsed anyway, so what felt like eternity was only just a second in human time. It felt complete and irreversible. Like something not of this world had happened and something that would remain untouched no matter what appeared to happen in my life. And wow everything was so full of energy. The stands in the hockey pitch were so alive, the birds that had gently started to sing were so alive, my body was beaming with light and everything seemed to be emanating with this one single energy that came from the source of silence of all that is. I had previously had powerful mystical experiences and had many since this event but none can relate to this single event. It is indescribable not because it was more profound or more mystical than any of the others but more because it just collapsed all ideas I had about life and myself to reveal the peace that has always been there. It was beautiful without involving beauty, profound without meaning to be profound and life-changing without changing my life. Everything broke down and yet everything also made sense at exactly the same time. And boy was I alive! I put the kit in the changing rooms and walked slowly back to my house in central

Exeter, full of the aliveness and still in a state of total none thought. Everything was so alive and nothing could disturb my sense of inner peace. Not the odd person I bumped into, not the fear of things related to the hockey (there is no fear in this state) and not the sense of needing to know anything (it had all gone in this state). It was the most beautiful and alive walk I had ever taken. That night I slept like a baby, with not a thought or comprehension of what had just happened other than I never wanted it to stop.

Chapter 2-
Annoyingly still very human

The profound state of silence didn't stay like that for long. More accurately I woke up the next morning to discover that 'Jack Prefontaine', with all his problems and worries still definitely remained, though there was this sense that it wasn't as real anymore and that at will I could tap into the silence that had been revealed on the hockey pitch. It was taking more of a back-seat though. In the moment on the hockey pitch and walk home after it had taken the central stage in my awareness but now it seemed happy to be much more of a back seat passenger and allow other things inside of me to come to the fore again. Despite at the time not having any questions (they were impossible in the state I was in on the hockey pitch), inevitably part of me was questioning what had happened. What was lucky was that despite reading a wide variety of spiritual books I wasn't wedded to any one spiritual idea, path or tradition that made my conditioning a lot stronger and hence it was a lot easier for the grace of silence to break through it all in that moment. I didn't need to worry though. The universe was fast going to start providing me with answers and as I was to learn over the next decade things always came into my life with very little effort when they needed to.

'So I started to experiment with human nature,' shared Sam, who was apparently a masters student at the University of Exeter. We had bumped into each other at the spiritual church (which I had randomly had a feeling to go to a week after the hockey pitch event) and had got a drink (a beer for him and an orange juice for me) in the local pub after. He was a very interesting guy. After a powerful experience after taking Weed one evening, Sam had started to question everything about human nature and was writing it all down in a little note pad he took with him.

'I wanted to do all these crazy things to test my reality of what was real and unreal,' Sam continued. 'When I had that experience that evening it was like my whole conditioning broke down and the fear associated with it also broke down, so I was free to do what I wanted.'

'Could you give me some examples?' I questioned in a curious manner, as his experience sounded a little like the experience I had on the hockey pitch. There was certainly no fear in that state. For a long time it had been apparent to me how conditioned people were and the small boxes we all tended to live in but it had become even more obvious after the 'hockey pitch incident' the week before.

'Well yes a couple of examples spring to mind,' Sam shared, scratching his long brown beard, which made him look very wise along with his long grey buttoned coat that covered nearly his entire body. 'Firstly I started to experiment with how I dressed. Like doing crazy things when walking around the shops in Exeter. I would sometimes dress as a middle-aged women, sometimes dress as an old man, sometimes walk around with nothing but my shorts on in the middle of Winter and sometimes walk around dressed in different costumes, like a policeman, a sergeant and a priest. Oh the look and stares I used to get,' he reminisced, laughing as he did so.

I laughed along, as it did sound like a crazy experiment and very funny. I had prayed last night for the universe to bring someone into my life who could help explain what was happening to me and although someone like Sam hadn't exactly sprung to mind (I was hoping for a bearded guru from India who looked like Ramana Maharshi), I had accepted he was the best messenger for me at this moment in time.

'I also started to experiment by playing loads of different characters. During the day I was Sam the normal economics and finance Master's student but by night I could be whoever the fuck I wanted to be. Two main characters I had lots of fun with. I enjoyed being the policeman and I also enjoyed being the crazy guy. With the policeman I have done all manner of crazy things like taking illicit bribes from pub owners to stop me reporting them, 'arresting' some hot girl and then trying to seduce her so we can have sex and also knocking on random people's doors and pretending I needed them as a key witness for a naked student who was causing havoc in the local Exeter area. This was so much fun but I also wanted to have some fun with the crazy guy. So I would sometimes stand with the multiple homeless people in Exeter and pretend to be crazy, shouting random shit at strangers and dancing around like I was mental, or sometimes I would walk into a shop and say the most outrageous thing to the person behind the counter.'

'Sounds mental,' I commented, not at all sure what to make of my new friend and very random messenger from the universe.

'Yes man it was so fucking freeing,' he replied, taking the last swig of his beer as he did so. 'If that crazy experience had taught me one thing, it is how we are just live in little conditioned boxes our whole lives. There is nothing to fear mate. Nothing what so ever. In that place I touched when I had the weed that blew my brain in half I realised that everything we think is real isn't really when you look closely at things. We are living in like a movie mate and are all just actors on the screen of life. We should be having so much fun, rather than stressing about all the little details, whether we are fitting in with the fucking crowd and what society has conditioned us to do.'

We talked until 12pm that night, as his insights fascinated me and were relatively well aligned with some things I had long thought. Definitely the part about the acting. It felt like people were always acting and playing prescribed roles to me but because they were so deeply in the human condition they thought it was very real and this is what caused all their suffering.

'Been great to chat tonight mate,' Sam commented, as we got to his house (which it turned out was only fifty yards from mine). 'You are truly one special motherfucker and I can't wait to connect with you again. Here you go take my mobile number and you know where I live now if you ever want a chat.'

It had been an awesome evening and I couldn't wait to chat some more. The next day I woke up early and thought I would send a Whatsapp to my new mate, just to say thanks for last night and arrange another time to meet up. I wrote the message and sent it.

'Unable to deliver message, number invalid' read a notification on the screen. That is funny I thought because I had already sent Sam a message on Whatsapp the night before to confirm numbers, which had worked perfectly fine. Perhaps it was the connection or something. After trying a couple more times during the day with the same message coming up, I decided just to go round and knock on his house instead. It was easy to remember since it was only fifty yards away.

'Yep,' answered a very good looking blonde girl who must have been in her mid-30s. She was dressed in a short mini-skirt and revealing green top.

'Hi my name is Jack, is Sam here pleased? I had a drink with him last night,' I explained. She gave me a warm inviting smile, raising her eyebrows as she did so.

'No Sam here,' she replied in a suggestive tone. 'Are you sure you were looking for Sam or did you just want to knock on the door of an attractive girl?' she questioned, raising her tone. I was very taken aback by this suggestion, as at this point I was still an innocent virgin and liked to think of myself as a pure living spiritual person.

'No, no, no, not at all,' I replied in a defensive manner. 'I'm not that sort of guy,' I tried to explain but she cut me off before I could go any further.

'You can save your bullshit for a girl who actually cares. I am so sick of stupid university guys like you thinking they can get to know me by pretending someone else lives here. Pathetic and immature,' she concluded, before slamming the door shut in my face, which was now red with embarrassment.

After much searching I did never manage to locate Sam again. I tried many more doors on our street, tried variations in the number he gave me and tried searching on the university email system but with no luck. Did he even really exist? I will never know the answer to that question but one thing that was certain is that he helped me a little on my path at the time. There were to be many more crazy events down the years, as you will discover in this book.

After the enlightenment experience five very clear things stood out to me and they never altered. There truly was no going back.

1. My system underwent a total cleanse so I could fully embody what happened

After the enlightenment experience the processes I went through are beyond the words one can write as a human being. It was intense, incredibly dark at points and amazingly energetically demanding. Everything that wasn't aligned with the light and purity of the silence of the enlightenment was going to get flushed out of the system- I had no idea 99.9% of it was there until the experience on the hockey pitch happened. It also certainly wasn't a quick process. It took many years for things to fully process and got to some sort of state of equilibrium, requiring me to do hundreds of sessions with others to help the process and stop me going totally insane. I was also extremely looked after by the universe. For the next 7 years after the enlightenment experience I never had to work a full-time job but was looked after from a financial perspective and in other ways too. It would have been impossible to live a normal life and go through the required processes. There was an incredible intelligence to the ebb and flow of my life, which was far beyond my control, as the universe sometimes stopped me working entirely to push me through some of the most intense processes or allowed me to work close to full-time occasionally to earn money or learn certain things on a human level.

2. All sense of being in control went after the enlightenment experience

It was very apparent to me after the enlightenment experience that the free will we are convinced exists doesn't in reality. I had no choice. I was happy to play my part in the cosmic drama and allow 'Jack Prefontaine' to enjoy life as much as possible but with an inherent non-seriousness and understanding that he was not the one in control of the direction of things. Another force had taken over entirely. From much enquiry into this I would suggest a certain amount of free will would appear to exist in the things that the universe doesn't really give a shit about (like whether you have weetabix or porridge for breakfast is hardly going to cause the biggest cosmic drama) but for the major things that are going to happen in your life there certainly is no choice. This is incredibly scary for our fragile egos but is also incredibly

15

freeing when understood at a deeper level. So many times incredible things happened in my life and so many times apparently catastrophic failures happened too but I was always able to look at it from a balanced perspective that fundamentally didn't really mind what happened anyway. It sometimes also triggered things a lot on a human level yet part of me could always be at peace too. As a final point it is worth noting that I would very rarely straight up tell someone there is no free will because it takes incredible spiritual maturity to be able to accept that perspective in one's life. Often I go along with the idea that people can 'manifest' things and they are the ones in control, as this is more initially empowering than believing you are totally at the mercy of a scary and dark world. However, as people mature spiritually I would encourage them to let go of this ultimately egoic idea and come to peace with less control over things.

3. **I always felt total safety on a deeper level**
The enlightenment experience revealed a place within me where things would always be safe. This was going to be very helpful over the forthcoming years as many dramatic ups and downs were experienced in my life, when I had to face some very deep darkness and when I had to go into situations that were completely unknown on every level. This safety had an interesting interaction with the human being. At aged twenty I was definitely a highly traumatised human being (especially in my body which I will detail later in the book). This meant it took a long time and lots of hard work to feel real safety in my body yet paradoxically I always felt safe on a deeper level no matter what appeared to happen. It was a total trust. It was like a beautiful light was always guiding my very strange life and would always lead to 'good things', even if the road there was often rocky and tough. It also always looked after me on a human level. When I needed money it was there, when I needed a certain type of relationship it was there and when I needed a break from all the spiritual work it was there. It was often very demanding and many times I would complain that the process was pushing me too far but yet I felt safe in the inner knowing that it would

never push me further than I could truly take. I was in safe hands that were much safer than anything the world could ever offer.

4. Spiritual gifts started to emerge at a rapid rate and then eventually disappeared entirely

After the enlightenment experience my subtle energy awareness started to open at a very quick rate. It was no surprise that very soon after the universe introduced me to my first spiritual teacher (via Jason), who had expertise in this area and could help me develop in the most appropriate way. It was much needed as often these things can cause huge problems. I quickly started to be able to feel energy beyond all proportion of what I could before, could read people at a very deep level from just meeting them or looking at a photo and had an amazing intuition where I could almost predict things were going to happen before they actually did in 3-D reality. It was quite scary at times but the work with the teacher and the fact that I stayed connected to normal life really supported me in staying grounded. Over-time I started to develop very powerful healing gifts. These sometimes resulted in some profound 'miracles' taking place, which were very 'spiritually showy' and were certainly good confirmation that something was happening. It all came naturally. I found the healing work natural when I learned to let go and trust my intuition. In fact it was often much easier and natural for me than normal worldly challenges most people in their twenties face. Then one day the universe completely switched everything off! It was very confusing at first and I was wondering if I had done something wrong but it appeared that I no longer needed any confirmation of these things and could be content with just sitting in a place of total trust. It was like going full circle. From just having normal everyday awareness, to developing bit by bit to have extraordinary mystic awareness and then just going back to normal again- there does seem to be some inherent lesson and maybe even a cosmic joke in this process.

5. I never really believed any of the spiritual books or teachers I had (I was unattached)

This point needs to be carefully explained. After the enlightenment experience the universe was clever in pushing me to search to heal some very human problems and trauma to make my everyday life better but at a deeper level all questions had really ceased. Working with many different teachers and paths, as well as training in multiple modalities was very useful. It gave me a much more detailed understanding of the whole spiritual scene and an incredibly comprehensive understanding of what was effective on the search for enlightenment. I was a strange student. Spiritual master after spiritual master was very impressed with me and so many people tried to tie me down to their way of thinking, their tradition or their spiritual school but I would always remain free. I always put one hundred per cent effort in and was very enthusiastic. This was often confusing for the person in charge as they often thought it meant I was very devoted to their way of seeing or doing things but in reality I was very devoted to being the best future coach to others I could be. Hence I had to be fair and put everything in to everything I did to see how it helped me but because of the enlightenment experience I was always fundamentally free from conditioning or attachment to one method at a deeper level. It helped me a lot when coaching my future clients. I firmly believe the worst teachers are those who only have one method or tradition to offer as what happens is they try to fit the student into the box, whilst in my coaching I wanted to help the client break the box and shine in their own unique radiance.

The paradox
Despite all these extraordinary things happening and me being able to touch the enlightenment as needed, the paradox was that the human being (i.e. 'Jack Prefontaine') fully remained. And he was a broken human being. Although I didn't fully know this at the time, deep self-enquiry, working with many people and a healthy dose of common sense would reveal I had been sexually abused as a young child. This had led to severe anxiety, digestive issues and also depression during my teenage years, as well as a total fear of intimacy and sex. I was a human being in need of a huge amount of healing.

As you will discover in this book, especially the chapters on sex and relationships, I made a fully recovery and eventually learnt to thrive in these areas. I have no doubt the enlightenment experience aged twenty helped a lot. It allowed me to hold the deepest pain and the deepest darkness in a space of complete non-judgement, as well as be able to see clearly that no matter how broken I was on a human level there was part of me that would also be eternally at peace. It led to many revelatory insights too.

Spirituality and teachers of enlightenment seem to either gloss over the human being or ignore the human aspect completely. This is bullshit in my opinion. My path and journey is a living example of how enlightenment merges with a human being- in this case a very young one (relative to most spiritual seekers) and also a very broken one (at least initially until the healing started to progress). I was a strange person. On one hand I lacked a huge amount of everyday confidence until I started to heal but after the enlightenment experience I was extremely confident spiritually. As time progressed I only became more confident in my spiritual insights. Due to my high level of mystic ability (as I saw by the multiple 'miracles' of healing that happened through me) I was never one to be intimidated in anyway by this side of things, which many teachers/masters/gurus used to their advantage to disempower their pupils. I was also extremely intelligent, so wasn't over-awed by the manipulation of words and texts that many teachers/masters/gurus also used to disempower people. And finally I also had many deep experiences working with a wide variety of teachers/masters/gurus, which revealed the truth behind the spiritual façade at an even deeper level to me.

I wanted to tell my truth.

This book is therefore not an idea, a concept or a search for enlightenment but an actual living account, with huge amount of valuable insights, of what it feels like to live a life after an enlightenment experience for the best part of a decade now. That is really the interesting part. Many spiritual teachers/masters/gurus celebrate an enlightenment experience like it is the end of the process and a separate part to your humanity. This book challenges that idea on the deepest level. There is no method or no guarantee when it comes to enlightenment (the grace of silence is the one in control), so really the interesting part is what happens after an enlightenment experience and more specifically what practical insights it can add to yours and other people's everyday human life. Practical, practical, practical- that is the interesting part if you actually want to do something with your beautiful human life. Therefore the underlying aim of this book is not to provide yet more speculation or intrigue around enlightenment but to provide something of tangible practical value, which can not only potentially transform your spiritual path but more importantly your everyday life.

And it is relentlessly honest.

Honest enough to tell the real truth when it comes to enlightenment and also honest enough to share my very human flaws/pain/limitations that make life just so much more worth living. This is highly empowering stuff. Although there are some very good teachers/masters/gurus out there the vast majority of them are no more enlightened than a jacket potato and after reading this book you will start to see past the bullshit to your own empowerment as the fucking awesome unique individual you really are.

Chapter 3-
Enlightenment explained

For the next six years after the conversation with Jason I dedicated my entire existence to enlightenment , until I realised it had already happened aged twenty on the hockey pitch. I just needed to get out of the way and let things process over-time. As such I failed epically in my 'perfect enlightenment' quest. I was expecting bliss, spiritual powers beyond belief, unlimited good emotions, nirvana and a state beyond human needs but all I found was a radical acceptance of my humanity. This definitely brought peace and also a gift for helping others. Eventually after much inner work spiritual people started to ask me for help in a wide range of things, which I would summarise as career success, loving relationships and vibrant health. You know human things. It was often coated in grand spiritual concepts, a search for "spiritual development" or "enlightenment" and X technique/lesson they had learnt off X guru/master/teacher but fundamentally when you stripped all the bollocks away this is what people really wanted. Or even more accurately they wanted career success, loving relationships and vibrant health from a place of radiant peace within.

All this searching and working with hundreds of clients gave me some radical insights when it came to enlightenment. Insights I had to share in a book. I honestly believe there is so much misconception around enlightenment and the spiritual path in general that not only blocks some sort of spiritual peace but also generally fucks people up on a human level a lot. This is a book that shares my truth. Ultimately one must always find their own answers but I hope at minimum this book points people in a decent direction and makes them question things that are actually doing them harm on a human level. There is so much exploitation, corruption and just downright lies in the spiritual world it is scary. It is completely the same as the corporate world bar at least in the corporate world there is a more fundamental honesty that this is about profit, power and control.

I am making no big claims about myself or this book other than I am more enlightened than a jacket potato and that if you read this book with an open heart you will be more enlightened than a jacket potato too. Now that is not to be sniffed at. Before jacket potatoes world-wide put in law suits against me for defamation I would like to place on record how much esteem I hold them in- they are very peaceful, very content, very honest, very flexible and very consistent. All qualities the vast majority of spiritual seekers, teachers/masters/gurus and the spiritual community in general lacks.

So what even is enlightenment?

Well this one is a tricky question! It is of course beyond words ultimately but what I hope to do in this section is to point you towards what it isn't and then from that foundation point towards what could be.

Enlightenment is not a personality. So many spiritual seekers and paths are stuck in this overt and often subtle notion that enlightenment makes you this great boring personality, full of gentle speech, meekness, an outer pervade of peace, not interested in the normal things in the world and this almost unconditioned God-like personality with no passion. Just think Eckhart Tolle for what I have just described. Probably a nice guy and certainly a decent teacher of being present but also up there with the most boring people to have ever lived. Does the guy ever smile? Does he ever show any passion? Does he ever show any real humour? Maybe I am being a little harsh but I am just trying to quite simply destroy this notion that his "awakening" has resulted in his "spiritual personality" when in fact it is just his normal boring personality from before that is still present. So many spiritual seekers and particularly the teachers/gurus/masters are living such a fake outer pretence, full of fake kindness, fake gentleness, fake compassion, fake seriousness and fake deepness, which gives people this impression that these things have a lot to do with enlightenment and one must behaviour like this to appear spiritual in the world. Nothing could be further from the truth.

Secondly enlightenment is not how you appear in the world. You could be a lawyer, the greatest spiritual teacher on Earth, a policeman, a stripper, an Olympic athlete, a painter, a singer or many other things (note people often define themselves by their career so we had to cover this first!). All that happens is your enlightenment infuses your career, pointing towards the inner realisation as you use your natural gifts and talents in whatever way is needed to function in the world. It also has nothing to do with your sexuality and intimate relationships (the second thing people most define themselves by generally!). You could be married, single, heterosexual/homosexual/bi-sexual, celibate or a lover of sex and many things more. It is totally up to your personal preference. You can also be any religion you want to be (the third thing people most define themselves by in the world). You could be an atheist, a Buddhist, a Christian, a Mormon, a Muslim, a Jew or god forbid even spiritual but again enlightenment couldn't give a shit. It is just your personal preference. You are free to choose.

Finally enlightenment does not take you beyond your humanity. There is a deep misconception that enlightenment will take you to this state beyond human pain and suffering, which is partly true but needs a strong explanation to fully grasp. The conditioned human being always remains. There will always be behavioural patterns, emotions (of the 'good' and 'bad' variety unless you really supress them all) and bodily sensations to contend with. What changes is two things fundamentally. By people able to re-connect to the enlightenment you become far more aware of what is really happening inside of you. And by God there is a lot! We have so many patterns of stored conditioned behaviour, with different charges to them (things that trigger you easily have more charge), which are made to create some sort of functional behaviour in the world. Evidently what you needed as a child to function is very different to as an adult. Yet critically the childhood behavioural patterns will never go away totally, you just choose not to use them and over-time their charge becomes much less if you don't engage with them for a period of years. Those people who are more unaware often play out many 'childhood patterns' in sometimes overt and obvious ways, whilst also playing out many that are harder to see unless you really deeply understand the full story of the individual. It becomes trickier to see this when people are very functional in the world. Although as a general rule you become more functional the more aware you are, sometimes people are just very functional in a specific domain and their childhood patterns would get deeply triggered if certain things of security were taken away from them. Some high-powered business executives, athletes and lawyers are good examples of this.

The second fundamental thing that changes, is that as well as becoming much more aware of all the different things that are happening inside, you can also sit in the part of yourself that I call the 'enlightened child'. Pain and suffering doesn't exist here- there is only a lightness, joy, peace and eternal purity. This 'enlightened child' is in all of us but most of us are so deeply disconnected from it, we allow ourselves to believe and act out endless patterns of behaviour that cause us so much suffering in the process. It is important to note that even a full re-connection to this doesn't stop the bodily sensations, emotions and thoughts, it just allows you to watch them and act out appropriate behavioural patterns with the joy and wonder of an enlightened child. There is still also some pain and suffering (seriously it is part of being human) but it is not 'my pain and suffering', which is the critical distinction. It is really the obsession with our disconnection from the 'enlightened child', which allows the very real pain and suffering we all experience to take on a whole new energetic form that makes it real pain and suffering. When watched fully with the "enlightened child" is still appears to be like pain and suffering but the texture is different.

The human condition

If there is one thing that enlightenment fully allows, it is a full understanding and acceptance of the human condition. It is so deeply woven into most spiritual teachings that enlightenment is all about escaping the human condition to this special place of 'nirvana or peace' but I challenge that very notion at the deepest level. In my experience it isn't true. Lets look at the 'enlightened child' and the human being, then explore how the 'enlightened child' interacts with the human being. This will then allow us to consider how behaviour is formed and question what morality really is.

The 'Enlightened Child'

As already discussed this is an unconditioned part of ourselves full of a lightness, joy, peace and eternal purity. It is in everyone. However, due to societal conditioning we lose touch with this aspect of ourselves very quickly and there is a dis-connection from the connection that never goes way. This is really important to understand. It isn't entirely accurate to say we have dis-connected from it (though it can be a useful simple teaching tool), as the reality is that it is still connected fully in everyone but most just can't access it.

The Human Being- body, emotions, thoughts, subtle energies

No matter how 'enlightened' or 'spiritually developed' one becomes the human being will always remain. So what is a human being? If we are being simple about it there are really four modes of experiencing reality- the body, the emotions, the thoughts and the subtle energies. Most people are aware of the first three and in theory as we start to open up more with our awareness we also gain greater access to the realm of subtle energies. I say in theory for a very important reason. As you read this book you will be perhaps amazed at my constant reminder in many different ways of the importance of getting into your body fully. The reason is simple. To fully experience both our emotions and the subtle energies we need to be fully in our bodies, as both operate in what I like to call the 'body-emotional' and the 'body-subtle' fields. Therein lies one of the great delusions of so called 'spiritual people'. Many believe they are starting to open up to the subtle realms because they can feel other's energy, they are practicing lucid dreaming, they are channelling energy in Reiki or they can feel the energy of a tree. Perhaps you can or perhaps you can't. Perhaps you believe it or perhaps you don't. It doesn't really matter. What matters is the subtle energies we experience through our very own 'body-subtle' fields, as this is where all the relevant information for us is. Including insights that will help our life. Similarly if you consider it carefully you can only feel emotions properly when you are fully in the body and hence the 'body-emotional' field.

This is why a lot of emotions often come up in sport, in a yoga class or after dancing.

Yet what about the thoughts? These are actually separate from the body/emotions/subtle energy fields and are the main way we block ourselves from the 'enlightened child'. Thoughts are neither good or bad. They often become maladaptive, resulting in sayings such as 'being stuck in his head' and 'lost in thought'. If you consider it carefully when you get deeply into the present moment of the body it is impossible to have a 'traditional thought' (which comes from past conditioning). You can have a 'present thought' when deeply in the body, which comes from more intuitive flow. However, this is more aligned with the body-subtle energy when deeply understood because by getting deeply into the body you allow yourself to be a channel for intuitive guidance to come through. Thoughts are needed in the human domain. You need them for a healthy sense of self (or a healthy sense of ego), using the mind intelligently to meet your own survival needs and function logically in the world. What often happens though is people, especially Western people, become very thought dominated. This is at the expense of the body-emotional and body-subtle fields, making us more disconnected from our hearts, the present moment and what is really happen on a subtle energy in the dynamics of any given relationship.

How the 'enlightened child' engages with each domain of human reality

The 'enlightened child' can not only function on its own accord, like a 5th way of experiencing human reality (only really in deep meditation when the other four domains become closed down), but it can also be accessed in each of the other four domains. It is like a watcher with attitude. Often spiritual people talk about bringing awareness to the body, emotions, thoughts, subtle energies and the awareness they talk about is like the 'enlightened child' I am talking about. I do, however, believe it has an attitude. Much like a child in that although they are generally pure and full of wonder, they do also tend to have a hint of an attitude about them. It isn't about morally. More like a direction that life itself wants to flow in through the domain of your human experience, accessing the body, emotions, thoughts and subtle energies to produce the desired outcome on a human level.

This takes a phenomenal amount of letting go and being prepared to go with the flow of life. It isn't a dissociative thing though. Often spiritual people get ruthlessly taken advantage of with this concept of 'letting go' or 'service for the greater good', where they really disassociate from the 'enlightened child' at best or at worst start to disassociate from some of their basic needs. The watcher with attitude, combined with a healthy sense of ego (mainly from the thoughts), would never let this occur. It is not spiritual nor necessarily always what you want on a human level. Sometimes it may put you in tricky situations or test your courage but with the underlying meeting of your basic human needs always present.

A question of behaviour

So given all of this how does this thing we call behaviour come about? Behaviour is really a conditioned response that uses the four domains of the human experience (body/emotions/thought/subtle energies) to create a functional pattern to meet the demands of your world. These start from the moment you are born and pile up on top of each other throughout life. No behaviour is inherently functional or dysfunctional, it is just needed to meet the demands of the environment at the moment in time. Perhaps the best example of this is trauma. Deep trauma, such as physical violence or sexual abuse, creates hundreds of patterns of behaviour to stop the body and mind fully feeling the effects of it in the moment. Although functional in the moment to stop the pain, these behaviours usually cause much later maladaptive patterns that can cause a person infinite numbers of problems with their life.

Each behavioural pattern has a certain energetic charge to it, which attracts experiences corresponding to the charge to us like a magnet and also hence makes it more likely that these patterns will play out. The only true way out of this is 'the enlightened child'. By bringing the purity and peace of the 'enlightened child' to behavioural charges and patterns that are causing us harm, they start to diffuse in their intensity and we ultimately

27

become a lot more free. Note that the 'enlightened child' can also be brought to behavioural charges and patterns that cause us a lot of joy. The effect here, however, is different. Rather than nutrify the charge, they almost give it a little more grounding and a better foundation for it to work its magic in everyday life. A final more advanced point is that we are not seeking to create only joyful patterns of behaviour- this would make it too directional and judgemental. It is more accurate to say we are trying to view the whole human experience from the gaze of the 'enlightened child'. Then nature works its' course. It generally has the effect on the behavioural charges and patterns as I have outlined but we can never say in totality, as you just don't know how things are meant to unfold. It is far beyond human comprehension but all one can say is that if you do bring the gaze of the 'enlightened child' more and more to the four domains of human experience then life is going to be better, more joyful and in alignment with the highest good for all.

A question of morals

One final point to consider before I share a personal story about what I have just described is the question of morals. There is no morality in the 'enlightened child'. Initially this is an incredibly scary realisation as our whole conditioning is based on the thought formed notion of 'right' and 'wrong' but when you go beyond this it becomes clear that there is actually more innocence from this state. A critical thing to see is that the 'enlightened child' is bringing joy into the world. So it is not as if this no morality suddenly leads you to becoming a bastard but what it does do is open you to the possibility that joy is not defined by your limited human definition of what is right and wrong.

Often the 'enlightened child' can be a little mischievous. It acts innocently and with a pure heart not of this world but sometimes this leads to people getting triggered into their own 'negative' behavioural charges and patterns to help demonstrate clearly to them what is stopping their joy. You will see lots of examples of this from personal stories in this book.

Going beyond morality also brings a lot more gentleness into proceedings. Firstly it helps you become a lot more gentle towards yourself, as lots of the guilt about 'doing the right thing' goes away and you can trust that if you aligned with the 'enlightened child' things are unfolding just as they are meant to. It also brings a lot more gentleness towards others. Of course there are things we all stand for as human beings and certain behaviours that are so misaligned from love that we could define it as 'wrong' but it certainly makes you a lot lighter on things that are far more petty and frankly insignificant in the grand scheme of things.

Watch for 'the enlightened child' imposter

The problem with all spiritual methods is that they quickly become a concept rather than an actual fact. The written word and other ways of sharing methods are always limited. What often happens is that when you share the concept of the 'enlightened child' or any other way to describe this 'place' within ourselves, the person who is trying to do the awareness creates a fake 'enlightened child'. This stops the process working how it naturally should.

How do you stop this fake 'enlightened child' becoming an imposter to your looking into the human condition and bringing more awareness to your life? There are three key things. Work with an experienced teacher who can help you become more aware of what is really happening and has your best interests at heart to empower you fully. Secondly meditate a lot more-particularly meditations that make it easier to embody the space of 'the enlightened child' more regularly. I actually don't feel it is that difficult to embody the 'enlightened child' quite regularly in meditation with practice…the tough part is doing it in normal life and being aware of it through the four domains of human experience. Finally get into the body, get into the body, get into the body. Most of the fake 'enlightened child' or fake 'awareness' problems come because the person is not fully and deeply grounded into their body, so they create a fake solution to block out body-emotional pain or body-subtle energy sensations.

Human ego and human needs

No matter how enlightened one becomes the human ego and human needs will always remain. This idea about going 'beyond

29

ego' and 'beyond all needs' is just a big fat guru lie to disempower people and keep them in a state where they can be easily manipulated. One should always have a good strong healthy ego, so you can meet the demands of your human needs in the world. The difference when you re-connect to the 'enlightened child' within you is that you can accurately see and use your ego for what it is- a thing to help you survive in the world, which should be used with intelligence without making a big attachment story about it. Making the ego real from a place of unawareness brings a lot of suffering. Yet making it unreal from a place of spiritual escapism or misunderstanding also only brings suffering. Hence choose the middle way. Use the ego intelligently to meet your human needs and have a fuck load of fun in life but never take it seriously at a deeper level in any respect.

Never walk into a shop called Enlightenment

A little story to share about how I found the main teacher who started to get me to look a lot more deeply into what enlightenment really was. He was the least glamorous of my teachers but certainly the best. If he was much better publicised I have no doubt he would be held in the same high esteem as Echkart Tolle amongst others (they both learnt off the same teacher Barry Long). A lot of what I share in this chapter was prompted by my work with him and I have then expanded on it to use my own terminology and experiences. He was the most honest teacher out there. So many spiritual teachers and gurus are leading you on about what enlightenment really is but he told it straight and was prepared to be almost completely unknown as a result of it. We will get more onto the current authority on enlightenment in the next chapter!

Firstly though I have to tell this story. It shows how much the universe was pushing to wake me up and you can never be sure where the best teacher of your life will enter from. Well I suppose in this case the name of the shop gave it away as you will soon find out…

I felt broken. My highly promising High Performance Sports Coaching career had ended out of nowhere a fortnight ago at the University of Exeter. One minute I was the most promising young hockey coach in England. The next minute I was a highly traumatised individual, who was suffering from some quite serious PTSD after a random unprovoked attack in public had deeply triggered long-held childhood trauma that I didn't know existed. I was unable to sleep, regularly having panic attacks and unable to function anywhere near the levels I needed to as a High- Performance Coach. I saw the truth of the situation quickly. This was going to take many months to heal if not years and to my deep regret (and fake masculine strength) I didn't want anyone to find out the truth, so I lied by saying I wasn't enjoying it anymore. My boss was shocked as a stand-out feature of my coaching was my utter passion and dedication but they kindly agreed to let me go in two weeks time after lengthy 'crisis talks'. Coaching for the next two weeks was an immense struggle. I was all over the place physically, mentally and emotionally but because coaching patterns were so deeply ingrained in my psyche could 'turn it on' for sessions and appear like my normal self, if albeit less passionate and as high quality as normal. Eventually my parents picked me up and I re-located to the relative quiet of their Cotswold home to face the biggest battle of my life.

A few months in I still wasn't ready to work again but was feeling better. I was still working intensely and regularly with my first spiritual teacher at this point, who Jason had introduced me too. I was making progress but it was slow. I had also tried traditional therapy but had found it way less effective and useful compared to the work I was doing with the spiritual teacher. Anyhow since I was feeling a little better I decided that I would go on an adventure. I chose Glastonbury for an over-night solo visit. This was a relatively random thing to do, as I didn't have any friends there and outside of the festival it wasn't the most exciting place in the world. It was, however, apparently the heart chakra centre of the Earth so that was my reason for going there.

It turns out that despite being the heart chakra of the Earth, Glastonbury was really just quite a weird dysfunctional middle-class town. There wasn't that much going on in mid-March time and the town itself wasn't very big at all. Containing a strange mix of spiritual stores offering anything from tantric massages, to tarot readings to intuitive art there really was any offering for any type of spiritual person. This was complemented by numerous small places to eat and a few B&Bs, one of which (The George Hotel) I was staying at. I soon realised it was going to be difficult to keep myself busy for much of the day. I had started firstly by climbing the hill to the famous Glastonbury Tor, before slowly making my way through the abundance of shops and very few people that made up Glastonbury Town Centre. I had a tarot reading, which proved rather fruitless and made up, before having a sandwich and packet of crisps from the local bakery. I was praying for some profound spiritual realisations to come my way. I had read and heard many miraculous stories of spiritual things happening in the Tor, so was extremely disappointed to get nothing better than an average workout from my efforts. I was planning to go up there again in the evening in case spirit was saving something profound for then.

After finishing my sandwich and crisps I made my way along the High Street, looking for an appropriate store to go into. One store caught my eye immediately. 'Enlightenment' was a small high street shop, with a maroon coloured front and the words 'enlightened' embezzled in gold across the top portion. It had a mixture of clothes, a wide range of tourist gifts, singing bowls, bells, clocks and many odd looking spiritual items. Immediately upon entering I was struck by the presence of an old man behind the counter. He seemed so focus, so still and so completely focused on what he was doing, which was watching the shop for customers coming in. He also seem weirdly undisturbed my by presence. Rather than say hello he stayed silent and I kept my head down, rumbling around the store along with the two other customers who were in there. Whilst doing this I kept being drawn to the old man behind the counter, like it was some of electro-magnetic attraction at work. I resisted as best I could but eventually shuffled to the far right hand corner of the shop, only two metres from the counter. I pretended to shuffle through some books (whilst mainly focusing on this strange old man) and picked up a random book. I turned the front cover to find out more about the author. Oh my God! It was the guy behind the counter! He had written a book. I quickly shifted to the back cover to find out what this book was about...'the book is transcribed from talks X gave on the subject of enlightenment, relationships and inner freedom. Most books about enlightenment tend to celebrate the experience of illumination as an end to itself. This book is more interested in what comes after such experiences, how they can be integrated and the attempt to live a life of integrity and authenticity.' Holy shit I thought! The guy behind the counter's gaze turned towards me, as his gentle but piercing presence went right into the depths of my heart.

I turned to meet his gaze. Immediately there was this incredible energy vortex between us (much more powerful than anything that had happened on Glastonbury Tor), as I felt a love not of this world illuminate my whole being. Although magnificent for a few seconds this quickly revealed my very real human pain. I felt my low levels of self-worth, deep seated feeling of rejection and total fear of really receiving love off another human being. I started to cry. Right there and then, in the middle of the shop. Luckily the other two customers had gone by this point, so it was just me and this mysterious man living it large and having some outrageous spiritual experience in the middle of a random high street shop in Glastonbury.

Classic and standard scenes for me and my weird life! He offered no condolences at this point to my crying, other than a gentle smile and a presence that invited me to be able to share anything with him.

'Can I have an appointment with you please?' I enquired once the crying had stopped.

Now at this point it may be tempting for the spiritually minded amongst you to think that I had met 'my guru' and all was happily ever after in Jack's spiritual wonderland. Nothing could be further from the truth! Although we arranged an appointment for the following week, I actually bailed on it out of fear and letting me current spiritual teacher down in the spiritual school I was in (more on that spiritual school later in the book). Eventually I managed to pluck up the courage to see him for a one to one appointment almost 15 months later, which led to me immediately leaving the spiritual school and doing a few more sessions with him. At a later date I also did a sequence of 10 sessions with him where we really did some deep inner work and I got a much more practical example of his method, which I added to my ever growing list of spiritual insights to draw from.

Working with him revealed many profound lessons, including to always be careful when you step into a shop called 'enlightenment'. There may just be an ordinary enlightened man waiting behind the shop counter for you!

Chapter 4-
There is no authority on enlightenment

The first big step one needs to take on the enlightenment path is to destroy this notion that there is any authority when it comes to enlightenment. I am certainly not an authority. And neither are spiritual gurus, spiritual masters or spiritual teachers, no matter how famous they are or how many followers they have. It is about being mature. There is certainly value in working with people to help you on the enlightenment path but it should never come from a place of awe, disempowerment or this notion that these people aren't somehow human too. From many different personal experiences I can share they always are!

The conditioning all starts in school
Why are we so conditioned to submit to authority? It all starts in school where we are extremely conditioned to believe there are right and wrong answers to things within a very limited scope of human awareness, that some adult authority figure has control over what we should and shouldn't know and that if we misbehave out of line then we will get punished by these adult figures and isolated from the community. The whole schooling system is totally insane and I could write a whole book on it.

For the purposes of this short section, however, the key point is that you seriously have to start becoming aware of how deeply this conditioning goes because it is the biggest blocker on the spiritual path. So many spiritual people want to "give themselves" totally to a master/guru/teacher, which can never work by the way. I question this whole notion of the 'devotional' path- it is a complete lie to disempower people and takes them in the opposite direction from some sort of inner authority, which is the beginning of maturity on the spiritual path.

School deeply conditions you to believe there is some sort of 'spiritual answer' that will make you safe and secure, just like answers to exams make you secure in the education system. This is all total bollocks when it comes to enlightenment. There are absolutely no answers for enlightenment, as the very re-connection with the 'enlightened child' reveals the answers are all really totally inside of you and that they are completely situational to the context anyway. This last point is critical. The school system teaches you only a very specific type of knowledge that is based on the thought awareness function of the human being, which can recount past knowledge that it has 'learnt'. Although one can use 'the enlightened child' in conjunction with the thought system this is the most difficult combination of the lot and takes years if not decades to hone. Instead enlightenment reveals a different way to give 'answers' in each context. Rather than it coming from pre-determined knowledge based on our past conditioning, as you become more aware you can train yourself to start to allow answers to come through you from the vortex of the 'enlightened child' which has answers far beyond the extremely limited scope of your past experience. When it comes to learning about enlightenment this conception is a vital point of understanding. Many so called 'seekers' are content with gaining more and more knowledge as the basis for their supposed spiritual journey to enlightenment but this has nothing more than a negative value, as it just creates bigger blocks to re-connecting with the 'enlightened child'. Any good guru/master/teacher should be trying to help you re-connect with the 'enlightened child' as the primary aim and just help you with your normal life as the secondary aim. This re-connection can come about through so many methods but never thought based knowledge. A certain level of knowledge is helpful to point you in the right direction, like this book provides, but after that foundation it is all about stripping away the trained reliance on knowledge so you can connect deeply with your own inner 'enlightened child'.

School also ingrains us to believe we need an adult authority figure to have control over what we can and cannot do. You see it everywhere in spirituality. Masters/teachers/gurus telling their students what they can and cannot eat, who they can and cannot hang out with, what disciplined practices they need to follow for so called enlightenment, what level of spiritual progression they are at and why their spiritual tradition is the best (and better than all the other shit ones out there!). We love an authority figure. It is also as a side-point why we are so deeply conditioned to believe that older spiritual teachers are more trustworthy and knowledgeable than younger ones, which is again a notion I question entirely. Like in all aspects of life, experience is helpful but often also leads to stagnation and a failure to keep on the edge of things. I had my first spiritual client when I was 24 years old- why not? Anyway back to the main point. It is vital on an enlightenment path that you let go of this notion that you need someone else to tell you what to do and not what to do- sure take advice from a trusted spiritual person who you have sought out to help you but they should always be encouraging you to access your own inner authority too. It is the same with discipline. Most spiritual people have far too much rigid discipline in my personal experience when they would be much better served by questioning the rigidity of their discipline and becoming aware of the turbulence within this is really hiding. A true sustainable discipline can only come from within anyway- not to impress anyone, not to prove yourself as worthy and certainly not to follow the orders of your teacher.

Finally we need to look at how scared we are of misbehaving and stepping out of line in context to our community. School teaches us we must conform or we get punished. Some brave souls choose to rebel against this within the schooling system but the most truly intelligent way is to do what you need to do to function in the world but rebel totally on every level within. Believe none of it! For example if I look back honestly at my straight A* and A grades at GCSE and A-level, as well as my 1st class degree I can honestly not remember anything I learnt and at the time thought it was completely useless too. I played the system and put enough work in but it didn't condition me. On a much deeper level I was never afraid to question the validity of what I was learning and whether the scientific truths, supposedly accurate history and subtle life lessons we were being taught were really true. It is the same with spirituality. Explore traditions that appeal to you, work with teachers that resonate and read up on the supposed truths of the spiritual path but never be scared to be the spiritual rebel. And the ultimate rebel is the 'enlightened child' within because it doesn't have an agenda or a direction. When you re-connect deeply to the 'enlightened child' you discover that nearly all of what you thought you knew about enlightenment and spirituality completely falls away, as well as what you thought you knew about life. Many people are rebellious because they are wounded. I propose you are an enlightened rebel. Someone who can enjoy and play lightly with the systems of the world but also someone who connects deeply to the 'enlightened child' within and believes none of it. How rebellious this makes you on the outside is up to divine direction, which is beyond your field of control.

Middle finger up to the three classic spiritual teachers

There are three clear types of spiritual teachers who appear to have a lot of authority in one way or another. I will detail the basic characteristics of each, then share a story from my own spiritual journey to explain more. The three classic spiritual teachers are…

- The teacher from the Eastern world
- The teacher from the spiritual gifts world
- The teacher from the enlightened world

The teacher from the Eastern world

Us Western people have a fear of the spiritual authority of people from the Eastern world. They appear more knowledgeable about ancient spiritual techniques, more likely to have learnt esoteric knowledge off their own master, more in touch with the ancient scriptures and just well more darn exotic than a white middle-classed English bloke from England who suddenly thinks he is awake. Although no doubt there are many authentic and brilliant teachers from both the Eastern and Western worlds, one must also judge a teacher by how much they empower you to connect with your own 'enlightened child' rather than the multitude of other meaningless stuff that we think gives a teacher some sort of authority. This was no more apparent than on my yoga teacher training…

'Secret techniques' from an Indian Spiritual Master

I was excited. I was well into my recovery from PTSD by this point and was now planning the next stage of my life, which I had decided was to be teaching yoga and meditation. I needed a qualification though. After much searching I eventually settled on an intensive 3 week yoga teacher training led by an Indian Spiritual Master (whose name I won't reveal since I am rather critical of him. I have not shared any true names in the book). He had sounded great on our first phone call where I had enquired about the training. I was used to the whole spiritual scene by this point and had just finished working with my first spiritual teacher, so perhaps this was divine intervention and now a real Guru had appeared after my initial training phrase. How wrong was I to be.

It didn't start great on the first evening that we got to the rural Cotswolds location for the training. On many levels. Firstly the Spiritual Master was nowhere to be found when it came to welcoming us, instead leaving it to his glamorous wife who was at least twenty years younger than him and apparently his assistant for the training. It only got worse in the night. For some reason they seemed to have miscalculated the number of people on the retreat, which left the four guys on the retreat crushed for space in the upstairs part of a converted loft. And the night only became more uncomfortable.

'Oh Donald Trump you are a wanker. God live the USA. Spank me harder Mummy. Fuck you naughty Women. Donald Trump is a wanker,' half-chanted and half-screamed one of the male retreat participants at about 1am in the night, waking the remaining three of us up. He wasn't moving as he talked but you could feel this incredibly negative energy presence coming into the room and he sounded as though he was possessed by something.

We each looked at each other unsure what to do with our new friend, until Jorik (from Poland) lost his patience with him and woke him up. This pattern continued another three times, before our designated wake-up call for a 6am yoga morning practice. It was fair to say we were all shattered by the time we got to the morning practice and determined to speak to the Spiritual Master to sort this out.

'You see it just isn't going to be sustainable for us to sleep in the same facility as him and with so little space,' concluded Jorik to the Spiritual Master, as all three of us talked to him after our first morning yoga practice. It had been fun, despite the lack of presence from the Master. I had been expecting a big divine presence full of love but all we got was a small reptile Indian looking man in a traditional Indian orange dhoti, who had a rather dead energy about him and rarely smiled, even when doing yoga.

' I see, I see, I see. Very difficult energy,' replied the Spiritual Master. 'We must find a solution to your problems,' he assured us. 'Rebecca, sort out this problem now please,' he instructed in a rather rude manner, pointing at his wife, who looked extremely glamorous in her tight yoga pants, short pink top and pink bun tying up her delicious blonde hair.

'What exactly is the problem?' she replied, moving away from her conversation with a couple of other female participants on the retreat in an elegant way to deal with our complaint.

'Stupid Women were you not listening,' retorted the Spiritual Master. 'Always the same chaps with this one- good at certain things but not other things,' joked the Spiritual Master in a chauvinistic way, which seemed mightly unfair given that Rebecca wasn't even part of the original conversation. Luckily for us Rebecca seemed used to his abhorrent personality, taking it all in her stride.

'I was just helping out these two lovely Females love,' she replied in a gentle tone that would have melted anyone's heart bar an angry Spiritual Master.

'Not good enough,' replied the Spiritual Master angrily, which was a state he was supposed to be above. 'You need to sort out of the rooms for the gentleman, as we have a problem with Mark again. Put him in the Caravan. Mark belongs in the caravan. Then these guys can rearrange their beds, so there is more space and it is more comfortable for them,' he finished, giving us a wink to let us know he was the man in control and could sort our problems.

'Oh I was worried about poor Mark,' replied Rebecca in a compassionate tone, fully of human empathy and worry.

'Don't worry it will be good yogic discipline for Mark to be in the caravan. He needs discipline and a more confined environment to truly thrive.'

We walked away with Rebecca to sort out all our rooms and tell Mark of his new living arrangements. Mark didn't survive long. Two days to be exact before the strenuous nature of the retreat and the pressure of confined isolated living became too much for a poor man with relatively severe mental health issues. Come to think of it we all weren't really sure why Mark had been allowed on the retreat in the first place. It was clear from spending five minutes with him that he was completely unsuitable to an intense retreat environment in every way, yet the Spiritual Master had still allowed him on (over-booking the retreat in the process) despite him coming to multiple classes with him previously. Perhaps it was about the money.

Things didn't get better in his esoteric lectures on the path of yoga and tantra. The actual physical and practical yoga teacher training we were receiving was fantastic, with it being led by a dedicated male student in his 30s of the supposed Master and also Rebecca, who was a fantastic teacher in her own right. The Master was above such matters though. His work was more concerned with our spiritual development, our understanding of the deepest truths of yoga and most of all our devotion to him.

'I want you all to take this orange bracelet off me one by one,' he instructed in the most sacred voice he could muster, giving the whole scene as much grandeur as was possible. I patiently waited for my turn in the line, unsure what all this fuss was about on only our second day there. I nervously shuttled forward. For some reason despite me being able to see through this spiritual fraud almost immediately, the reverence and aura around the word 'Spiritual Master' still seemed to have a lot of control over me.

'Hi, how you doing mate?' I asked as I got ready to receive the orange bracelet off the master. For fuck sake Jack why did you call him mate?

'No questions,' instructed the master, looking deeply into my eyes with the intent my Dad used to look at his bacon sandwich in the morning. It was powerful stuff. 'This orange bracelet ties us together for all of eternity as master and student. I am here to support you with your spiritual development, your spiritual purification process and for your ascension into the light,' he stated, with almost a grand tear in his eye. He certainly was a showman.

Now I wasn't really sure if I had signed up for this in the terms and conditions of the retreat but I decided not to be a spoil sport and played along like it was some sort of grand initiation. Some of the other participants were generally worried other. Were they really tied to him to life? Had he used some sort of yogic magic on them? What if they didn't want to follow him in the future? I told them not to worry, as the reality was it was a meaningless bracelet that was only symbolic in nature. I had got ridden of mine immediately after.

The next day after the young male teacher and Rebecca had shined, we were left with another profound lecture from the Master to consider.

'Let me just tap connect to divine guidance,' shared the Master in his usual attention seeking method, as he lent his small oval head back, pressed his finger against the third eye position (between the eyebrows) and started to shake like some profound message was entering him.

I could see through the utter bollocks. I was already two years into training with my spiritual teacher in an advanced mystery school at this point, so knew 'divine guidance' could pour through you in a much more down to earth and natural way. I could feel the Master was really disconnected anyway.

'Yes there are the words the divine has shown me to share with you all lucky students today. We need to look into the history of tantra. Now before I start I need to be careful not to over-load your beautiful minds with too much information from someone who has a doctorate in this subject. My guru used to say me I was an unfair person to be around. It was because I was not only very beautiful and attractive to the Ladies but I had so much intelligence that the top University in India gave me a scholarship when I was only 16. And I studied the history of tantra, producing a much well read and appreciated piece that was praised all over India.'

He sounded very convincing as he was saying this but we had absolutely no way of knowing if any of this information was true.

It felt as they he may be applying poetic licence to some parts. He continued with his 'divine' lecture on the history of Tantra for the next hour, which admittedly was quite interesting if a little lacking in structure and precision. Perhaps this was how 'divine guidance' came through. After finishing his lecture and answering some questions, which required even more intense 'tuning in' apparently, he had one final incredible offer to make us.

'Now what I want you all to do is go deeply into yourselves. The master wants to help you get more in touch with your soul and its purpose. In two ways. Firstly master would like to offer a free, yes a free, soul reading to help you understand the energies you have to work with in this lifetime. These normally cost five hundred pound. Secondly we are now going to use secret techniques to access the primary energy coming from your soul.'

He proceeded to talk us through some grand process for the next twenty minutes, before he finally had put us up to the main point of the exercise.

'Now in deep trance and with purity of intent I want you to ask your soul what energy it most resonates with. You may get an image initially but what we are really looking for is a word'

I wasn't quite in deep trance by this point but managed to come up with the word 'peace'. He then asked us all to feed back our enquiry one by one. Part of me was tempted to play a practical joke and report back that my deep soul enquiry had revealed my primary energy was one of a 'dickhead' but this felt slightly inappropriate to the grand scene that was being set-up by the master. One of the participants did report back in all seriousness that their energy was a 'clown', which the master seemed to think indicated a gift with humour to inspire others. This seemed a very generous interpretation to me. At the end of the class he asked to see us each briefly one by one to set-up our soul reading appointment if we wanted it. I was curious to how he was managing to charge five hundred pounds for one of these readings and it seemed far too much of a good opportunity to turn down, so I willingly signed up despite my reservations of the master by this point.

'Destiny brought us together today,' shared the master in an authoritative tone, as we sat down on a secluded bench a couple of days later to discuss the findings from my soul reading. I wasn't sure if it really was destiny or the fact that I had manged to find a couple of thousand pounds to go on his yoga teacher training retreat but regardless I nodded along and played his game.

'This will be the most important and revelatory reading of your young adult life Jack Prefontaine,' shared the master in a powerful way. 'It will be like nothing you have ever had before, despite the spiritual work I know you have already undertaken,' he shared, sounding slightly threatened by me working with others.

'Looking forward to it,' I replied, gazing deeply into his eyes and showing him that I wasn't intimidated by anything he through it.

'Right,' said the master, 'Lets begin.'

He then lent his head back and closed his eyes, which I think symbolised he was tuning into to divine source for the reading rather than having an impromptu mid-afternoon nap.

'I see a lot of energy around you Jake Prefontaine. A bright spirit, yes a bright spirit. Full of positivity, full of laughter and full of joy. Yes, yes. I think maybe one day you become a very powerful yoga teacher. Yes, yes, yoga teacher. Your destiny was to come here to learn off the master, so you could takes your first steps on this profound journey towards your destiny of being a great yoga teacher. I even see you working for the master. Yes, yes, Jake Prefontaine working for the master. Maybe just more in the administration to start with and then as your yoga practice and devotion to the master grows, you can start to teach. Just like Rebecca and Matthew, you could one day have the privilege of working for the master.'

This surprised me. Despite normally being full of chat and happy to answer back to my superiors, I was literally dumb-struck. Not because this soul reading was opening some incredible opportunity for the master with me but because this had to be the biggest loads of shite I had ever listened too in my entire life.

'Now, now,' continued the master, 'we need to look at the other key energies in your life.'

I nodded my head on agreement, perplexed as to where this was heading.

'Do you have a girlfriend?' asked the master. I shook my head, so he offered a suggestion. 'Ah perhaps young Jack Prefontaine can get with young Angela from the retreat- she is a very special soul and it could be a divine union under the watchful and all knowing eye of the master.'

'I'm ok thanks,' I replied, having no sexual or personality attraction to the hippy Angela whatsoever.

'Ah, ah, just a suggestion,' replied the master. 'People often say no when I offer my visionary solutions but over-time master is often proved right.' I didn't reply, so he continued his enquiry into the other key energies in my life. 'Now do you have a sister?'

'I do, just the one and no brothers,' I shared.

'Does she had the boyfriend,' he enquired. I wasn't particularly sure why whether my sister having or boyfriend or not impacted me in any profound way but I answered that she did. 'Good, good,' continued the master. 'I have a divine suggestion. Yes it comes through very strongly now. She I think needs a relationship reading from the master with her boyfriend- slightly more in-depth than the normal soul reading but because you are a dedicated pupil of mine, I do it for only three hundred and fifty pounds instead of the normal seven hundred pounds. You tell her right?'

I nodded my head in agreement, whilst secretly thinking of how ridiculous my younger sister would think I was for thinking she would spend anywhere near that amount of money on some random reading from a supposed spiritual master from India. She seemed happy enough in her relationship to me and would probably prefer to spend that sort of money on a holiday or something.

'Now, now,' continued the master, 'how is the relationship between your mother and father? Very powerful energy your father has. So powerful I think it would be over-whelming for the Mother. Am I right?' he enquired with a cheeky know it all grin, which suggested he was used to being told he was right about everything.

To be honest I didn't think my father had that powerful energy- they seemed to have a pretty balanced relationship to me.

45

But why even argue? I nodded my head on fake agreement, opening myself up to the inevitable.

'I have another divine suggestion,' continued the master. 'Master thinks that your mother and father also need a relationship reading. Same special price because of your relationship with me as my student,' he enthusiastically pitched to me. I nodded my head, indicating that I would speak to them.

'Is there anything else for me to learn from my reading?' I questioned slightly impatiently, wondering what fool would ever pay anyone five hundred pounds to be told they just needed to be their student. As well as that, all I had learnt so far was my sister and boyfriend as well as my mother and father also needed readings from the master based on divine guidance he had received.

'Yes, yes. There is one more very important thing. I have noticed a slightly rebellious and non-conforming streak in you Jack Prefontaine, which likes to challenge authority, particularly mine. Now I was a rebel too when I was younger. But over-time I learnt to respect my elders, especially my master, as I am to you.' He paused for a moment, letting his hurt and strong words go deep into my soul, before delivering the knock-out blow. 'Where is your orange bracelet?' he questioned, with a frown across his head and a look of disgust in his reptilian looking eyes.

'I got rid of it,' I responded boldly and confidently, as I was tired of his shit.

'Traitor!' screamed the master. 'You will never be able to access the secrets of tantra with that attitude Jack Prefontaine,' he scolded, pointing his index finger at me. I remained silent, so he continued 'I will give you one more chance to go on this unique journey with me. Of course, however you respond you will be able to do and complete the yoga teacher training but what I am offering is a chance to touch the mystic, the unspoken and slowly but surely share the secrets I have learnt from some of the greatest masters in India.'

I agreed to one more chance, intrigued to what he would say.

'Ok, I can see you are a very special pupil. Much more advanced than the others,' he commented, trying to appeal to my spiritual ego. 'I am going to teach you an advanced secret technique to help you go deeper within and be less of a rebel, who doesn't recognise his own master. Now what I want you to do is firstly open your mouth and then extend your tongue, so it touches the top of your mouth behind your front top teeth.'

I did as instructed, unsure as to what was the point of this.

'Now close your mouth, still breathing through the nose. Can you speak now?' questioned the master.

I shook my head, making funny noises as I did so, to indicate that even if I tried to speak I couldn't because my tongue was stuck to the top of my mouth.

'Excellent, excellent,' shared the master. 'Now what I want you do is keep practicing this secret technique regularly throughout the retreat, so you become an expert in silence and it destroys the rebellious streak that doesn't love your master.'

I nodded my head, whilst secretly thinking he had to be one of the biggest wankers alive.

I did manage to complete my yoga teacher training and enjoyed at times further winding up the master on the retreat through my non-compliance. He was an extreme example of a bad spiritual master/guru. Although he was never my direct teacher in any single way, he had a large following and his abuse of 'spiritual power' was a prime example of how readily people are to give themselves to someone who appears to hold the keys to the secrets of the Eastern World.

The teacher from the spiritual gifts world

People tend to be very impressed by spiritual gifts as a sign of enlightenment and a trusted teacher to follow. We see it all over the spiritual world. People training as Reiki Masters, in soul reading techniques, in energy healing modalities and our obsession with psychics/astrologists/tarot readings. We love to feel special about ourselves or that someone else has some sort of specialness that will give us more control over our own lives. That is not to dismiss spiritual gifts. It is certainly true in my experience that different people have different gifts, which should really be measured by how much they help other people with practical things.

So what do spiritual gifts have to do with enlightenment? Nothing really, though it would appear to be true that as one opens up more spiritually then certain gifts that weren't there before to come to the fore so you can help others and really at a deeper level learn more about yourself. It is also worth noting the 'gifts illusion'. Many people in the spiritual world are obsessed with collecting more and more gifts to their ever growing spiritual ego, when in reality most people with self-awareness start to develop a lot of gifts that are beyond normal functioning. The more down to earth don't have an obsession with naming and claiming it though. They are happy to say they got 'lucky breaks' (rather than being obsessed with their own manifestation), that they use their 'intuition' (rather than clairvoyance/clairaudience/clairsentience/clairalience/clairgusta nce) and that they 'have a feeling' (rather than a connection to spirit or X ascended master or angel). I feel down to earth language is better. It takes a lot of the spiritual escapism, specialness and bollocks out of it, as well as making you approachable to a much greater range of people (bar the ones with massive spiritual egos that are best avoided anyway).

As already shared at the ripe old age of 21 I was very lucky to be introduced to my first spiritual teacher by Jason. This spiritual teacher was part of a mystery school. It was a prestigious school that had been developed after the Spiritual Master in charge of it had been gifted 'a light' in 2005, after training as a Reiki Master amongst other things. He had then trained other practitioners in it to work with clients, with the school having worked with over 20,000 people by the time I joined it. This Spiritual Master in charge of it was impressive. Not only had he developed this revolutionary spiritual method but he had also developed to the point where he could deliver Darshan, being one of the first Western Gurus to ever be able to do this. He was the real deal in many ways. Certainly from a spiritual gifts perspective it didn't get much better than that and working with his process through one of his practitioners helped me a lot, as well as eventually training as a practitioner in the school and working with my own clients. There were flaws though. Despite his incredible gifts the spiritual master was certainly a human being too, which was very helpful to observe in shaping my own opinion on spiritual gifts and enlightenment. Below I share a visit he made to Exeter Uni to deliver Darshan when I was 22 (which was an incredible experience), along with an experience that helped me see his very human side too.

Darshan and 'divine selection' from a very gifted spiritual master

It was all coming together. After much hard work I had successfully managed to organise a Darshan event with the spiritual master for eighteen participants crammed into a room in Exeter community centre. It was a rather unusual event for the centre. Rather than the normal language classes, poetry classes, posture and mobility groups, warhammer club and meditation classes they had somehow allowed me to host a Darshan event with a Western Guru that promised to be rich in extraordinary experiences for the participants. It was also a rather unusual event for someone just finishing their degree to host. Rather than going out celebrating with my mates (admittedly I didn't have many) about the end of exam, my focus post-exams had instead been to organise this very rare event with the spiritual master. The light was coming to Exeter! It was a very rare thing, as he only offered a maximum of five Darshans a year and as a spiritual community we were unsure only long he would continue to offer the live Darshan for. Darshan was an interesting process. It involved you going up one by one to look into the spiritual masters' eyes, with a phenomenal amount of energy transferred to help you on your spiritual path. Each participant usually took about two minutes if not longer when they went up.

There were three main people involved- myself, the spiritual master and the head of the spiritual school (who had been my teacher since I was introduced to him by Jason). We had the privilege of sitting at the front of the room. The rest of the participants were seated in a circle, some nervously making polite conversation with one another and most staying in their own private space to mentally prepare for what lay ahead. Before the participants had arrived the spiritual master had gone out of the room. Not only to surely add intrigue and a little mystery around him but also to prepare energetically for the great demands on him that lay ahead. He wasn't quite as gifted as avatars like Mother Meera who could deliver Darshan with no apparent effect on their body or energy levels. The Darshan took

49

a lot out of the spiritual master. It was my job to go and collect him when all the participants had their eyes closed in meditation, so he could take his seat and deliver the Darshan one by one to the participants. Once he was in the room I would tap the participants on the shoulder one by one to go up, with everyone expected to keep their eyes closed until instructed when the Darshan was over. The idea behind this was to help people go within and stay focused but I suspect it was also to add a little intrigue around the mystery of the spiritual master too.

'All ok with you Jack?' questioned the spiritual master, as I entered the private room I had hired for him to prepare in. By God did he look sweaty. I actually felt quite sorry for him, as the subtle energy poured through his body and was obviously having a massive impact on his heart. He was used to all this though. He made a funny joke at his own expense and indicated he was ready, so we walked to the main room where all the participants were waiting. It was a little like guiding a blind person at this point. The spiritual master was rather in the zone, as his long grey hair and rabbit looking face, remain fixed on the floor in front of him and I nudged him on the shoulder of his smart buttoned white shirt to make sure he didn't crash into the wall at points. We eventually entered the room. I felt a little like an undercover agent at this point, as I guided the spiritual master to his seat at the front of the room and had a quick word with the head of the spiritual school to make sure operation Darshan was ready for action.

It is hard to describe the immense light and amazing experiences that happened over the next hour. Although I eventually left the spiritual school and am no longer on speaking terms with anyone from it, the experience of hosting a Darshan in Exeter will always be one of my most treasured life memories. It was an incredible feeling. When it was eventually my turn to receive Darshan, which I had already done on three previous occasions, the feeling of complete peace and clarity of purpose was beyond description. It wasn't quite like the experience on the hockey pitch. That was all-encompassing and broke it all, whilst this experience was more a gentle softening of that initial process and a final confirmation that everything was going to be ok. The event went well too. All the participants seemed very happy with what they had received, many people bought extra things from the spiritual master after (one should always have their business hat on) and I already had half of them signed up for a repeat Darshan later that year in Exeter. It was a great success and I also hosted a very successful one later that year.

My reputation was fast increasing in the spiritual school. I was now the head of the spiritual school's star pupil and was now a trained practitioner, being the youngest to ever train in it by around fifteen years. I was the next big hope. The spiritual master and the head of the spiritual school seemed very disappointed with the effort of the twenty-five or so other practitioners, bar a couple of them (with one of these being the spiritual master's partner). This seemed like a crossing of relationship boundaries and this interesting relationship was going to cause me lots of problems going forward.

The tension had been building for a while. After going on a retreat with the spiritual master's partner I was very unhappy with something that had taken place on it and was seriously thinking of quitting the spiritual school. Then came the next 'evolution' of the spiritual school. The spiritual master liked to think of himself as a cutting edge spiritual revolutionary, which in all fairness was probably quite legit when you had brought a new spiritual method into the world that over twenty thousand people had used. The latest development was going to cause a lot of tension in the school.

As already shared there were around twenty five practitioners in the school using the method of the school to help people heal and develop spiritually. There was this main school that my teacher was the head of, another sub-school using a slightly different method that the master's partner was head of and then the master himself. He was mainly focusing on delivering Darshan at this point in time. The new method was going to be a more simple version of what practitioners were already doing and the aim was to make it more appealing to a bigger audience. This sounded exciting and I wanted to be part of it. The problem was that despite helping organise a couple of Darshan events for him my relationship was not strong with the spiritual master and he didn't seem to like my potential to up-stage as a bigger deal in this very small sub-sector of the very small spiritual world.

After lots of patient waiting, I eventually decided to ask my teacher (the head of the school) directly about whether I was going to be involved or not. The response wasn't positive.

'You see Jack your just not trustworthy enough in his eyes and don't have the right vibration to hold this new form of light,' he explained to me. I was taken aback but assumed my teacher would at least be involved and perhaps over-time I could work my way into things.

'I assume you have been selected though?' I questioned.

'No I also don't have the right vibration,' he replied matter of factly, before sharing that the master's partner and four other women were the only ones going to be selected at this stage. He seemed to accept it all at face value but I could smell spiritual bullshit a miles off.

'Doesn't have the right vibration,' seemed a convenient spiritual escapism to get around some difficult truths around this whole thing. More like doesn't have a vagina and a complete devotion to the master, with an unwillingness to question anything would have been more accurate. The whole thing made no sense on two levels. Firstly he had selected practitioners who were barely working with any clients- if they were unable to get clients using the original method, it seemed stupid to trust them with this new method. Secondly I had a massive issue with it from a business perspective. I had invested a lot of my own money in training as a practitioner and now they were going to effectively going to massively de-value my investment by creating a whole new competing method that was going to become the new focus for the school. I raised both issues. On the first issue I was told I was projecting my own issues around Women onto his decision (the projection excuse was always a key method for them and many other spiritual teachers/gurus I have seen). Let's just skip around the obvious human facts and make it all about the student's issues, like the teacher/guru is this perfect being and above such petty human biases. Total bullshit and always will be. On the second issue I was told I should focus on being more devotional to 'the light' and focus on doing what I could to 'spread the light' in the world. Always a convenient excuse not only used by this spiritual school but many other teachers/gurus too. Again it is all about the avoidance of general common sense human concerns by making it about service to this apparently divine thing that just screws you over on a human level. The best example of this is when gurus/masters are making millions, whilst convincing followers of them to do volunteering work as a means of service to their mission of Earth. What utter bollocks and exploitation!

It was safe to say that after getting these responses I wasn't staying in the spiritual school. When one has invested so much time and effort into a path it can be extremely difficult to let go but from a session with the enlightened man in Glastonbury I was able to see the truth a lot more clearly and find the courage to move on. After this the spiritual school closed ranks on me, like all communities/cults do, with no-one prepared to talk to me from it.

The teacher from the enlightened world

After the experience at the spiritual school I was determined to only work with the best going forward. The spiritual school had helped me a huge amount on many levels but like all things in my life the universe always intervened when it was time to move on, often causing problems and making things much more obvious for me. I kept working hard. Firstly I worked with the enlightened man from Glastonbury for a number of months, including a brief break to go on the fated yoga retreat with the Indian Spiritual Master, before I decided to move onto a new teacher (a spiritual master from Hong-Kong). I wanted the real deal and this man offered it. He was a best-selling spiritual author, had created unique methods of yoga/Qi-Going/Tai-Chi to help spiritual seekers and I had felt an instant resonance when I had watched him talk at a Course In Miracles event. I signed up for a one to one intensive with him over a number of months.

So far my work with him had helped a lot. It wasn't exactly revelatory but I found his focus on normal life refreshing, as well as his methods very practical in helping me raise my vibration and embody what had happened to me when I was twenty years old. It was progressing so well that I started to full trust him. About three quarters of the way in he decided that to take the next step on my spiritual journey I needed a new name, to help me let go of the past and embody fully the new vibration he was leading me into. This is quite common in spiritual practices all around the world. The spiritual master from Hong Kong had himself changed his name when he came over to England, to help make him more approachable for his students and ultimately fit into English life better. He explained the intention was different for me. I needed a new name because 'Jack Prefontaine' was not powerful enough in his eyes and to really break free from the past he wanted to give me a name he had been guided from spirit.

'Your new name is going to be Jay-Jay Masters,' he shared with me, after giving some background context. I have to be honest that I was hoping for something better. It sounded like I was a disabled bird with a keen interest in golf- surely I could have hoped for more! But no Jay-Jay Masters it was.

'Do I have to use it everywhere? Even when people already know me as Jack?' I questioned.

'Yes of course Jay-Jay,' he replied, emphasising my new name again just in case I had forgot it in the last five seconds.

'Even in my hockey coaching?' I questioned further, not exactly convinced that the Oxford University Blues teams I was coaching at the time would respond well to a sudden name change from the coach half-way through the season.

'Yes in all contexts Jay-Jay,' he replied firmly. 'You should be proud of your new powerful name,' he re-assured me. I was very pumped up and enthusiastic about all the work I had been doing with him, so I readily agreed without really thinking it through.

The following day I found myself in front of the Oxford Blues Ladies team, ready to give my normal team-talk before our match.

'Right girls, if we all listen up,' I stated in a firm tone, to stop all the chitter-chatter and ensure they were all focused on the words I was going to say. I took my normal deep breath to compose myself and did a subtle Qi-Gong posture with my hands to make sure I was as centred as possible, pausing for effect before I started to speak. I had a master plan to carefully introduce Jay-Jay into the hockey world. It hadn't gone well the previous evening when I had introduced Jay-Jay to my parents but perhaps that was to be expected when they had chosen my name at birth. I was hoping the university girls would be an easier crowd.

'Just a little bit of admin to start,' I shared, which was a common occurrence before we got into the details of the match. 'As you know we have no game on Wednesday, so we will be having a rest from training on Monday. So even more reason to work at one hundred per cent today.' My plan had been to start with something hockey-wise to get them relaxed and into the flow of things, before casually introducing Jay-Jay like it wasn't a big deal at all.

'Also just a more personal point from me,' I continued. The vast majority of them looked up quickly at this point, almost sensing something was slightly off and this was going to be different from normal hockey team talks. 'From now on you can call me Jay-Jay,' I instructed. A look of disbelief quickly spread across their young faces. 'Everyone in hockey has always called me it, probably should have mentioned it before, but now seems like the best time to break cover,' I concluded, trying to add a little bit of humour into what only was ever going to be a humorous situation. They all burst out laughing apart from the Goalkeeper (always a special breed), who looked even more confused than normal. Inevitably a million questions followed, which I tried to answer and bat away to the best of my ability. This led to a delay and we were fifteen minutes late getting onto the pitch.

It was safe to say we didn't have the best performance of the season in the first quarter of the match, as their young minds were much more focused on the sudden name change of their coach than the opposition in front of them. Luckily we somehow managed to stay at nil nil and I could then re-focus them for the second quarter. The Oxford lot certainly had a sense of humour though. I (more specifically Jay-Jay) was voted 'dick of the day' and I had to write a match report as punishment. In Oxford tradition a match report was never a factual report of the actual match but a made up report on some random intellectual thing that related to the team, with the aim of being funny to the other members. I went for a detailed analysis of names in the ladies Blues for my match report. I mean what else was possible after the introduction of Jay-Jay? My match report had a look at the various characters of Jack and Jay-Jay, before scrutinising members of the Ladies Blues team. It was great fun and was well received.

It was safe to say the name change spread like wildfire in the hockey club and the Men's Blues team were already wise to it long before our next training session. It provided much good banter and humour for the rest of the season for us all.

After trying with Jay-Jay for a month I decided to put the poor lad firmly in the name dustbin, never to be mentioned again except in this book or by annoying Oxford Students who used it as banter for the rest of the season. What did it teach me about the spiritual master from Hong Kong? Well my opinion of him was still very high- he had helped me a lot and was certainly an enlightened human being. With big emphasis on the human being. You see although I could tell from his aura that he was a fully realised being, I also knew form first hand experience that he was still conditioned like all enlightened beings are. The name change had worked for him, so he was conditioned to believe it would work for me. It was honest well-intentioned advice but was ridiculous and funny in the effects it had on my everyday life. It really wasn't needed- I could just continue being plain old Jack and perfectly normal. One more funny thing stood out. The spiritual master from Hong Kong was normally extremely disciplined- a proper tai chi/qi-gong/yoga master who had a ridiculous level of energy and health for someone in their 70s, always on perfect time for all my sessions and so focused in what he was delivering to me. Except one session. In this session I had to wait outside his house for ten minutes because he had been up late socialising with friends from the night before- he was still very professional and it was a great session but it just goes to show how extraordinarily human these people could be sometimes.

This experience was a very valuable one. It taught me what I had suspected and the enlightened man from Glastonbury had always shard with me- that no matter how enlightened one is, the human being always remains. There were of course many frauds in the spiritual world to varying degrees but this spiritual master from Hong Kong certainly wasn't one of them. He was amazing in so many ways and a great teacher. He just also happened to be very human still, like all the rest of them! And sometimes gave crap advice too! Considering how much he had helped me though I was very happy to let him off in that one and to be honest I had quite enjoyed my little adventure with Jay-Jay Masters in the world.

A Note on Famous Teachers

As well as the above three types of teachers who appear to have authority on enlightenment perhaps the most powerful authority is the teacher/master/guru who has many followers. Their fame would appear to give them authority. It makes the average spiritual seeker, generally devoid of much intuition and certainly devoid of the ability to see an aura, more secure because they don't have much else to go on. It is of course a ridiculous notion to think someone's fame gives them any authority on enlightenment. The vast majority of more public teachers are really just supported by a very good business structure and people.

I would like to mention a couple more famous teachers to hammer home the point- two at opposite ends of the spectrum in Tony Robbins and Ramana Maharshi.

Tony Robbins is the self-help guru of the 20th century. He has had a massive positive impact in the world, helping huge numbers of people improve their everyday life and getting amazing levels of success in the world. He is all about progress. What he is not about though is enlightenment and in all fairness he never claims to be, though there is of course a subtle hint within all his teachings that this is the true way to freedom, peace and happiness (which is what some people may consider as an enlightenment of sorts). Enlightenment would reveal a different way. When you tap into the 'enlightened child' all need for progress and even purpose falls away, to reveal the radiant peace for accepting things as how they are and how they unfold in the world. That is not to say you should just sit on your arse doing nothing though! On a human level (which is definitely part of the picture if we are going to embody an enlightenment experience) we do need a certain amount of progress and also purpose to bring meaning to our lives. Being able to tap into the 'enlightened child' takes all the suffering, striving and pain out of this process though. We can just see things how they are. Often gurus like Tony Robbins and some other highly successful people who I have actually directly worked with are very disconnected from the 'enlightened child' and hence they have to achieve so much in the world to hide away from the huge pain and confusion of this dis-connection. Re-connecting to the 'enlightened child' allows you to have a more gentle meaning and progress, which is more whole and comes from a place of peace within rather than a massive state of lack (despite what Tony Robbins and other similar gurus like to say on the outside).

Ramana Maharshi is the non-duality king of the 20th century- the one all the non-dual people (generally the spiritual group most focused on enlightenment) love to hold up and admire as a fully realised soul. The perfect example of an enlightened man. I have a different, slightly cheeky opinion, which vividly demonstrates the key focus in this book on the interaction between the 'enlightened child' and human being. Before I begin to get myself into trouble I would just like to share I feel Ramana certainly was a fully realised soul. Doubtless he inspired many spiritual seeker towards true freedom and his mere enlightened presence was enough of a catalyst for serious spiritual transformation in people if the stories are anything to go by. He was also, however, seemingly a very fucked up human being. I mean seriously what sort of person spends years on a hill without taking any notice of the outside world? He must have had quite a severe mental health condition initially within his humanity to go along with his realisation of the 'enlightened child' within. Things did improve for him and he eventually apparently became active in the Ashram that grew around him. Yet even then I believe one should aspire to higher levels of embodiment in the real world- quite frankly an ashram in the middle of nowhere in India is very far removed from the ordinary Western world. Although many liked to point towards his simple living methods as a sign of his enlightenment, I just feel it shows a poor Indian person who wasn't able to live his enlightenment in the Western World. This therefore isn't that helpful to a Western person who has to live in the modern world and would also like some sort of enlightenment.

The courage to stand alone

We eventually now get to the key point of this entire chapter-the part I have been trying to make your heart open to by destroying one by one all the different types of authority that people cling to on an enlightenment path. I want you to have the courage to stand truly alone. Of course it is intelligent to be mature and at points on your path work with people you feel could help you but inside you must always seek to be totally alone in your own authority. Only you can decide!

There is much need for human relationships, human community, human intimacy and human love but they do not need to be part of your spirituality and enlightenment. Just let them be part of your human life. What spiritual seekers always do is confuse their human needs with those of their 'enlightenment needs', seeking spiritual community, spiritual friends and spiritual love to replace the dearth of this in their normal everyday human life. This is all fine and well but confusing it blocks the enlightenment very quickly. Always be an outsider to the spiritual and enlightenment worlds. I mean always go right in fully into any method with all your heart (otherwise you are not giving it a fair chance to transform you) but always with an intelligence that you are not wedded to one method, one teacher or one community other than your loving family and friends. The enlightenment accident becomes much more likely then.

I have no idea how much you are resonating with this book, how much you like me at this point or how much you agree with my ideas on enlightenment but one thing for sure...I had the courage to walk alone at many points. And I would implore you to have the same courage because it is only be being fully prepared to stand inwardly alone in your own 'enlightened child' authority and strip all the fake protection away that you can truly be free. There is no authority but you in the whole of existence.

Chapter 5-
Enlightenment and
Spirituality

What does enlightenment have to do with spirituality? It turns out not a lot. Initially for around the first five years after the enlightenment I considered myself a spiritual person, going up all the way from just plain old spiritual to mega spiritual. Then I dropped it all.

Let us examine three main types of spiritual concepts from the perspective of enlightenment. Firstly we will look at the 'super attractors' who manifest all their desires through the power of their mind, then we will look at the 'special channels' who have access to angels, enlightened beings and sometimes even God directly to give spiritual messages to humanity and finally we will look at the 'positive and peaceful Pollyannas' who can remain positive and peaceful no matter what is happening in the world.

Never trust a super attractor

'Super attractor' is a term I have stolen from the spiritual teacher Gabby Bernstein, who it just so happens I quite like actually. She is grounded, practical and fun. Along with a number of other prominent teachers they love to share the benefits of mindset hacks and manifestation techniques to help you 'attract' your desires and get you the life you deserve. Before I examine this from the perspective of the 'enlightened child' two disclaimers. Firstly it is an intelligent thing to talk about from a business marketing perspective- people in this domain are by and large very life improvement focused, so if you talk about things that help them get more money, better love in relationships and the career they dream of then you are making yourself attractive to a broader range of people. The second disclaimer is I feel that these sorts of teachings are very helpful to the vast majority of people, so although one could say they are superficial they are really what the vast majority of people need to improve their life. So no harm being done and no manipulation like the masters/gurus- just some good old solid spirituality in action and kinda cool how many people are now getting interested in this sort of stuff.

From the perspective of enlightenment, however, one needs to be radically honest about the value of these teachings. They tend to take you away from the 'enlightened child' within you. Firstly the underlying foundation of these teachings is that there is something wrong with you or with your life, which needs to be fixed and improved upon. There is nothing wrong with wanting to have your human needs met. These teachings, however, tend to take this to the max and make it all about constant improving, constant striving and quite frankly a constant underlying dissatisfaction with what is. And often in a very sneaky way. They will get you to say things like 'I attract the love I deserve', 'I deserve only the best' and 'I love myself fully, universe show me the way', as well as highlighting how it is all about setting your intention and then sitting back to let the universe bring the manifestations into your life. So it appears as though you are letting things flow naturally and there is an ease about it all. Yet seriously when you see it clearly it becomes obvious how much underlying striving and frankly stress there is in all of this- such a focus on what is happening in the outer world and subtly the message is that you can only be happy if you get what you desire.

Enlightenment has a different way. By fully re-connecting to the 'enlightened child' within you it becomes obvious that you have absolutely no control over what you manifest into your life- the directionless direction of the 'enlightened child' is really the one in control. This is very scary for 'super attractors' to consider. Initially it is empowering in one's spiritual journey to believe in manifestation and your own 'super attractor' ability, as it at least at minimum gets you to turn within and re-discover some sort of inner power rather than believing you are constantly at the mercy of the world. For deeper progress though the whole 'super attractor' idea needs to become totally redundant. Throw it in the spiritual dustbin and burn it into a million pieces! The truly empowered 'spiritual person' realises they are not the one in control- they can sit in a place of inner radiant peace no matter what appears to be happening in their life. The universe will eventually test you as your enlightenment path progresses. Often people experience 'beginner's luck' where lots of things will flow and things appear to manifest very easily, as the universe teaches you that perhaps there is some sort of power that you had never considered before. The 'super attractors' always get stuck at this point and believe in their own human ego idea that they are the one's manifesting it all and it shows how powerful they are as the creators of their own experience. I mean like seriously how self-centred is that? Depending on divine flow the universe will then often strip away this idea often very forcefully and painfully- no matter how hard you try to manifest your desires, the universe will keep making things go wrong until you accept that actually the power is not yours. This is an advanced lesson.

Overall there is a lot to learn and be grateful for from the teachings around manifestation and being a 'super attractor', as it helps people improve their practical everyday life and empowers them. I always saw it from a different perspective. I only discovered these teachings after the enlightenment experience had already occurred, so for me they are always somewhat baffling and it was easier to see the limitations within them. Enlightenment reveals a different way. Rather than being a 'super attractor' one can accept oneself as an ordinary human being and let the directionless direction of the 'enlightened child' be the one in control. This brings proper peace, allowing a lightness and ease of grace that the 'super attractors' will never discover until they let all their ideas and concepts about manifestation go.

Pretending to be a super attractor to manifest a six figure business

There was a point in my life that I was very determined to make lots of money and create a six figure business (with the sneaky long-term hope of making it a seven figure business). I decided to get expert help. I worked with a highly talented Woman, who was about my age and an expert in helping people create six figure businesses. From the outside she seemed to have it all. She had a large social media following, was doing extremely well in her own seven figure business and was amazingly attractive too.

She was also a big fan of manifestation and the law of attraction. A large part of the attraction (if you excuse the pun) of working with her was that she put a big focus on mindset and raising your vibration, rather than just business methods. I had fallen into this trap when doing business courses before. Working with very disconnected people, who were obsessed with making money and had scant regard for how to balance that with some sort of connection to the 'enlightened child' within.

I really went for her methods one hundred per cent like I always did. I made audio recordings with background music of me chanting a load of affirmations to myself, with phrases such as 'I deserve to be a millionaire', 'I attract abundance into my life' and 'I love money' featuring strongly. Everyday I would listen to them. I would listen to them upon waking, I would listen to them when doing my exercise and I would listen to them before going to bed. I was certainly thinking about money a lot is all I can say.

I also did all the other exercises she suggested, coming up with a unique programme to sell to people. Sell, sell, sell was always her focus. And I was starting to get results, with eight free breakthrough calls within the first two weeks of working with her. There was a problem though. I kept attracting people who didn't want to invest in my hefty programme fee of £4,997 she had suggested. Couldn't blame them to be honest! I sought some advice and was instructed to focus on my sales pitch, as well as creating new affirmations around how I only attracted 'paying clients'. All the affirmations were starting to hurt my head by this point. It also felt very disconnected from the 'enlightened child' to always be so scripted with everything and trying to force life so much. I kept persisting with no results, so we scheduled an emergency coaching call.

'How are you?' I asked her, just trying to make some polite conversation at the start of the call.

'Absolutely great,' she replied. 'Feeling positive, feeling focused and feeling ready to help you smash through your inner blocks to get the money you deserve Jack,' she shared, almost trying to convince herself of her positivity. I could sense she was a little upset and the energy between us seemed to be starting to open up her heart more. I was not going to say anything but felt pressed intuitively to probe a little further.

'I feel like you're a little upset?' I enquired gently. She seemed initially slightly taken aback that I wasn't playing the standard client-coach script but then relaxed and was able to share honestly from the heart.

'My Mum just puts so much pressure on me,' she replied, as a sad look spread across her beautiful pink lips and her blue eyes looked a little gloomy. I knew her Mum was heavily involved in her business. 'For my recent interview with Jack Canfield I was so nervous. She was so obsessed with making everything perfect and it is just so much pressure when you are running a business like I am.' She started to cry, as her guard came down and I saw the vulnerable young girl behind the powerhouse of a business Woman. I was about to console her, question some more or offer some advice but had a strong feeling just to say silent.

'Right but anyway this session is all about helping you sell Jack,' she continued, changing her tone to more business like and putting the vulnerable girl firmly back into the box. 'We need to change your mindset and get you your sales script right. I want you to make six figures this year Jack.'

We proceeded with a normal session but the rare flash of vulnerability had exposed what I was starting to see clearly. Perhaps this investment and desires for my business had been a lesson all along. So many people who were famous or very successful in the personal growth/spiritual world were actually trapped and unhappy on the inside. They deserved a lot of admiration for their success but it often left them disconnected from the freedom and radiant peace of the 'enlightened child' within.

I never did sell an expensive programme and was perfectly comfortable with it. I was much more interested in pursuing my hockey coaching career, alongside working with the occasional client who was committed to progressing on their enlightenment path. This made me happy and was aligned with the directionless direction of my 'enlightened child'. This connection is all we should ever be aiming for and you can be rest assured that your human needs will then be met too. Not always in the way you imagine or perhaps a sneaky part of your conditioning requires but in a way that will certainly bring you radiant peace.

'Special Channels'

Perhaps there is no better example of people trying to escape their humanity by being 'special channels' for a wide variety of spiritual creatures. We have people who channel certain ascended masters, people who channel aliens from different planets and even people who directly channel God. Very impressive from afar. Especially when these people seemingly channel beautiful words that uplift our spirits and enrich our hearts with love.

I deny all channelling. To me it is simply an attempt to create a duality between the human being and something more mysterious, in an egoic way to ironically pretend to take the ego out of it. There is a fundamental lack of honesty. If wise spiritual people are to be believed there are always angels, ascended beings and spirit guides overlooking us, perhaps even giving us intuitive messages and allowing us to 'channel' higher messages. Maybe this is true or maybe it isn't true. What is certainly true though is that if anything is going to come into the earth realm it takes a human being to write it down or speak it- an ordinary breathing human being with all its imperfections and insecurities, who is going to shit in the toilet everyday if they have normal bowel movements. Nothing magical happening there. Lets look at the three main types of things people channel (ascended masters, aliens and big man God himself) to consider why people feel the need to do this one by one.

In the spiritual world people are very obsessed with ascended masters. Apparently they are high-vibrational beings of love and light, ranking at the top of the so called spiritual hierarchy. And in the word hierarchy we can start to discover what this is all really about. If there is one thing that the vast majority of people (spiritual or not) are scared of it is their own authority and as such they then project this fear by looking for an authority figure outside of themselves. The ascended master is a sneaky authority figure. Sneaky because it goes beyond the human authority that spiritual people like to pretend they don't need, instead putting in authority in the place of a divine being who is completely perfect and completely not human. This is clever. When one becomes more awake you quickly discover it is foolish to completely put authority in another human being but the perfect enlightened ascended master offers a nice escape out of this, whilst still having some authority. It becomes even uglier when one then becomes a channel for an ascended master. This is a very blatant attempt to use the authority of this perfect enlightened being to make yourself appear better and more authoritative. I mean seriously is the enlightened ascended master benefitting from a human channelling them? Do they get paid? Do they get more followers? Do they feel better about themselves? It is so obviously just a marketing ploy from people who are scared of their own inner authority but still desperate for some type of spiritual authority over other people, so they use the enlightened ascended master to get it. So I say laugh and say fuck off to all the ascended masters. Throw Jesus, Mary Magdalene, The Mother Mary, Buddha, St Francis, Vishnu, St Germaine and the rest of the gang in the spiritual dustbin because they have no authority whatsoever.

We then move onto the channelling of aliens, such as the arcturians, pleiadians, galactic council, lyrans and many more. This is basically the same concept as above. The only difference is this time we have a tad more humility- instead of channelling perfect enlightened ascended masters we now channel aliens who are definitely more spiritually evolved than us but maybe not as perfect as the enlightened masters. They are still desperate to talk to humanity though. And always from different dimensions of reality- sometimes 5D, sometimes 7D and sometimes even 9D if we are really lucky. If they were really that spiritually evolved wouldn't they just come into 3-D reality? A lot of excuses are made in this regard, such as our reality is too dense for them and they can't interfere in our free will but my guess is that it would rather destroy the channel's business and sense of importance if the aliens just did it themselves. That is probably the real reason.

Finally perhaps the ultimate channel is the one who can channel God directly. This is perhaps best known publically in the 'conversations with God' series but there are many other examples of people claiming to be able to channel 'God' in public. The first point is that it is quite unclear who this God figure actually is. Quite why God, who is impartial and loving to all, would decide to channel messages through certain beings remains unclear but one can only assume he wanted that individual to massively profit off it. He is definitely a very loving God to that individual. When we examine things deeper perhaps the truth is that the people claiming to be able to 'channel God' were scared of just saying it was their own thoughts, as that wouldn't be quite so magical, mysterious or special in the eyes of the public. It is again a clever marketing ploy. It plays into people's natural obsession to get answers from this so called 'God' figure and makes it appear elevated and many even pure, when in reality it is just a human being writing their thoughts down. Doesn't quite sound so spectacular then!

Mary Magdalene is not my biggest fan

Towards the end of my time in the spiritual school I signed up for a self-love course with the spiritual master's partner. She had recently become a 'channel for Mary Magdalene's light'. The ten month self-love journey was being jointly offered by both her and Mary Magdalene, with the aim of helping participants discover new levels of self-love for themselves. It was kind of Mary to join the party. I had been on a Divine Feminine retreat with this Woman and Mary's light in the summer, finding it powerful and quite transformative. So I was excited to see what impact it would have on me.

The first few months went well but then spiritual politics problems started to occur. Having decided to leave the spiritual school for problems already mentioned with the spiritual master (her partner), I was in an awkward position of whether to stay with the self-love journey or not. In the end finances dictated. I had paid over one thousand pounds to be part of this unique opportunity, so thought I better see it through to the end. I did, however, let her know I wasn't going to go to the in-person grand finale at the end of the self-journey because I felt uncomfortable being surrounded by so many people from the spiritual school (of which this self-love journey was heavily associated). I awaited an email reply.

'Dear Jack,' the reply started. 'Myself and Mary Magdalene have decided to withdraw your privileged opportunity to take part in the self-love journey. I hope you can see that your actions in not wanting to be at the in-person event at the end of our journey are not only disrespectful to me but also Mary Magdalene and her light. We have both decided to offer you a partial refund to compensate you for the months you will no longer be able to take part'. I could only laugh!

It was lucky the self-love journey had managed to have some positive impact on me by this point, as it wasn't the most uplifting news to be told that even an enlightened being full of perfect Divine Feminine love wasn't the biggest fan of me. I mean not only did the Women running the self-love journey feel offended by my actions but so did Mary Magdalene, who felt disrespected and maybe even belittled by what I had done. What a bastard I was! Yet seriously this has to be the best example ever of people hiding behind channelled enlightened beings to escape their own human decisions and frankly their own human revenge. She wanted to get back at me for leaving the spiritual school and this was the perfect opportunity.

'Positive and peaceful Pollyannas'

The final spiritual concept that the spiritual world is full of are the 'positive and peaceful pollyannas'. They are everywhere in the spiritual world. They entice you with their positive thinking, high vibration and most of all bewitch you with their unbelievable ability to remain peaceful no matter what. Sometimes they can also be quite passive aggressive. Reminding you (in a rather forceful) tone that you shouldn't have negative thinking when you dare to express a fraction of honesty and also reminding you to not show very human parts of yourself where you dare to express some real emotions that don't quiet equate to their version of how peaceful a spiritual person should be.

Enlightenment bursts the bubble of the 'positive and peaceful pollyannas' and reveals truth. By connecting to the 'enlightened child' you discover two critical things where the 'positive and peaceful pollyannas' are concerned. Firstly in the 'enlightened child' there is absolutely zero notion of positive and negative- that would apply some type of moral judgement, which simply does not exist in this form of dissolved awareness. All thinking is just thinking and all emotions are just emotions. They only become positive and negative through the stories we attach to them and how we play them out in the world. There really is no need to unnecessarily discipline oneself through making yourself think positively or by only expressing positive emotions- in fact this often leads to distortion and an inner storm of powerful 'negative' thoughts/emotions just ready to burst out onto an unwilling target. It also takes so much energy. If emotions and/or thoughts are coming to the fore that we would normally term as 'negative' the best way to stop them having a permanent and long-term hold is to allow them to work through your system (not project and play them out into the world but just allow). This allowing, however, can only come through a deep recognition that all thoughts and emotions are ultimately ok on a deeper level and there is no need to judge oneself or anyone else for that matter.

Secondly by connecting to the 'enlightened child' alongside the recognition of the human body, thoughts, emotions and subtle energies we see that peace can only come about through allowing all to flow. It is not some fake pseudo peace that the pollyannas love to project (whilst facing turmoil on the inside) but is a real living breathing peace that can flow fully with life. And accept all aspects of the human experience, with no need to create an image or stop an aspect of the very human side of oneself flowing fully.

A final fuck off from the spiritual school

I promise this will be the last time I share a story from the spiritual school in the book- it was a rich experience that helped me grow so much but also one that showed me so many funny and limiting aspects of spirituality very clearly. There was an 'Elder' in the school who was the perfect example of a 'positive and peaceful Pollyanna'. She was always so positive about everything on the retreats we went on, as well as appearing so peaceful and kind to everyone who was on them. In a sort of over the top way though.

Anyway who would send me a nasty and aggressive email when I left the spiritual school? Of course it would be the

Pollyanna, who just couldn't keep up the fake pretence anymore and let loose with how I was 'walking away in fear', 'I was a disgrace to the people who had helped me in the spiritual school' and the best one at the end of the email that 'she wished me the deepest blessings on my spiritual path'. I mean like yes slag me off and basically tell me I am a total wanker but at least end on a positive Pollyanna note. She obviously just needed to let loose and I didn't take it personally. It was the perfect example of someone who was always trying to put on a positive and peaceful outer bravado in her spiritual setting to make herself look good but as soon as someone broke ranks the real feelings and human being came out full force. Not pretty scenes!!

Article from my friend Jag Reeves (https://www.jag-reeves.com/)

As a final little bonus to end this chapter with, I just had to share a fantastic article from my friend Jag Reeves. Jag was also an exile from my old spiritual school. He is also someone with extensive knowledge of the spiritual world having trained in multiple modalities and worked with hundreds of clients over the years. We did the below article as a little challenge (obviously very non-competitive since we are both super spiritual), with my article one of the thirty I share at the end of the book.

10 Naughty Things About The Spiritual World I Would Tell A 10 Year Old

Let's say that we broadly define 'naughty' as badly behaved, perhaps with a cheeky or even twisted element to it. We'll keep it light, humorous and a little silly to appeal to the young mind of a 10 year old, yet, we'll include a few darker and sharper edges to satisfy the adult mind in its scrutiny of everything spiritual…

1.   Some spiritual people believe that they are actually not fully human, sometimes even not human at all. Or they are born of a human race from long ago… such at Atlantis (the aquatic, fish people – relatives of mermaids and mermen) or Mu (pronounced Moo though without any relation to cows). Others are part pixie, some part dragon. Then there are angel humans. Occasionally you may meet a human leprechaun, and if you are really lucky you could meet an alien human, from many light

years away, who has come to be on earth by some sad and unfortunate accident...

2. Many spiritual people believe that there exists a spiritual world separate from the 'normal' everyday world in which most other people live. You can access this spiritual world only through the use of special tools and techniques such as meditation, lucid dreaming, shamanic journeying and chanting. If you are blessed to know a high vibration spiritual master, they can give you a special access, fast track pass to the spiritual world. It's like flying on Aladdin's magic carpet. Which leads into the next one...

3. Spiritual people are better than normal people. It's just like the story of Harry Potter – you have the wizard children (the best ones) and then you have the Muggles (the ones no one wants to be – they're like peasants). Spiritual people are a small but elite group of The Chosen Ones, people with amazing gifts and qualities. They have been chosen by God for a special mission at this time. God is like Santa Claus only ten times better. He doesn't wear red though. He prefers white as it better shows off his purity.

4. Spiritual people are ranked accord to their power. You have the junior Spirituals and then you have The Masters. The juniors always seek out the Masters because they have all the answers to all the spiritual questions. Masters are very special and very rare beings. They can often be tough on the juniors but every junior knows it's worth going through the pain. Every junior secretly wishes to be a Master one day. It's like the dream of owning Mayfair and Park Lane in Monopoly.

5. Spiritual people are very sensitive beings. The longer one remains a spiritual person, the more sensitive one becomes to everything not spiritual – often referred to as 3rd dimensional reality. Spiritual people live only in 4th and 5th dimensional reality (or higher) where they can be more connected into the truth and oneness of everything. This means they have no time

or space for mundane things like office work, politics, tv, beer or football.

6.   Life is now an urgent process of ascension. The planet is ascending and taking us all with it, whether we like it or not. Humanity is on the brink of disaster. Now is the time to step up to the spiritual plate. This means spiritual people have to work hard at increasing their vibration. They do this through two means – eating the right spiritual foods (which means no meat!!), reading the right spiritual books, practicing daily yoga and meditation and devoting themselves to their spiritual master. The other vital component is avoiding everything which lowers a spiritual person's vibration...

7.   Your spiritual vibration can be lowered by being around the low vibrations of unspiritual people. Low vibrations are to be avoided as if they were a spiritual Covid-19. No spiritual person wishes to be infected with the bad vibes of unspiritual people and places. Sadly, sometimes even spiritual people can go 'low vibration' which is when they have to be put into a spiritual quarantine and sent away for a 2 week raw juice fast meditation retreat.

8.   Spiritual people cherish freedom above all else. It is believed that normal people, like sheep, are happy to be imprisoned within their hamster cages, perpetually keeping the hamster wheel moving. Not so for spiritual people – they demand a life where they can do what they wish and when they wish it. This means wearing very baggy, multi coloured clothing (usually with a mandala print), dreadlocks, or at least long hair and hanging out on a tropical beach somewhere. They can be likened to a race of Peter Pans and Peter Panellas.

9.   Every Peter Pan dreams of meeting his Peter Panella. And vice versa. The Twin Flame is the pinnacle of the romantic fantasy ecstasy. This is that one person who will complete you. They are your equal, the Queen to your King. Forget about soul mates, they are so second grade now. The Twin Flame will take you back home, into the unity of the oneness of life. In reality,

the Twin Flame will crack you open, rip you apart and leave you a dribbling, incoherent mess. This little detail is overlooked and ignored in the dream. Until the dream is shattered.

10. Spirituality can fix all problems. If you are experiencing a lack of money, then you have to create a bigger and more abundant vision board. You must meditate more deeply and for longer so that you may increase your powers of manifestation. The same process is applied when seeking for the Twin Flame, the perfect spiritual vocation (that demands no more than a 5 hour working week) or finding the most aligned spiritual community to live in. Focus and intention bring results, that is MANIFESTATION. This makes spiritual people extremely self-obsessed indeed.

Chapter 6-
Enlightenment and Sex

Now I have given you a board overview of my background and the concepts around enlightenment I have discovered, we are now going to explore it all in everyday life. This is the pinnacle of an embodied enlightenment to me. It is relatively easy to connect with the 'enlightened child' in a remote cave in India but this book is for modern people who want to live from a place of radiant peace in everyday life, so we therefore have to look at how it works in modern life. And what better way than to start with sex?

Apparently as a man I am supposed to be thinking about it multiple times a day and I am pretty convinced Women (even the spiritual ones) think about it a lot too. Yet most of spirituality seeks to avoid it!! It is always the elephant in the room- everyone knows it is a big part of life but everyone seemingly wants to avoid talking about it in case they look unspiritual! Apart from in tantra. There it has to become this ultimately spiritual thing, which is used for total transformation of the human being and heck maybe even enlightenment. I propose a middle ground. A book that talks about it honestly and openly in the context of enlightenment but not one that has to be make it this super spiritual thing- it's just a good old human fuck (with a little bit of added awareness from the connection to the 'enlightened child' within).

Sex was something I learnt a lot about. No not because I was some massive stud but because it was something I was extremely traumatised around and frankly scared of for a long time because of the childhood sexual abuse already mentioned. I knew what it felt like to have had an enlightenment experience but also completely disconnected from one's sexual energy. This led to some powerful discoveries and plenty of funny stories to accompany it too.

I feel the sexual energy is a critical component of life- a big reason why many of the spiritual masters/gurus/teachers often lack a real enjoyment and teach a lot of things that are about going beyond the world is that they are disconnected from a flowing sexual energy within themselves. The sexual energy encompasses a lot. It generally leads to a much better flow of money in your life, allows you to have firm boundaries in relationships and allows a connection to a real love for life (especially the pleasures of it).

Not making sex a bigger deal than it is

There is an easy temptation to make sex a much bigger deal than it is. All we are really looking for on an enlightenment path is the ability to make sex an enjoyable part of one's normal life, experiencing fully the pleasures of it and accepting the different sexual kinks that one may have. Of course one may also remain celibate but it should never be out of suppression, a spiritual ideal or to 'remain pure'- it should instead be viewed simply as a lifestyle choice. Tantra tries to go the other way and use the sexual energy to transform the human being. Not the worst idea since we are so naturally focused on it anyway but often an idea that blocks the 'enlightened child' because it then makes sex this sacred and spiritual thing it was never meant to be. It is simply just a down to earth human thing. Of course, like all aspects of life, one should try to re-connect to the 'enlightened child' during sex to bring the maximum amount of awareness possible to all the human aspects of it. Yet probably best not to over-think it either.

You might as well try to enjoy it to the max

Having now accepted that sex isn't that bigger a deal, perhaps we can just relax and try to enjoy it to the absolute max. There is a lot to be said for the healing potential of pleasure and how it makes you feel so much more connected to enjoying life to the maximum. Why are spiritual people and people seeking enlightenment so obsessed with going beyond this world? Those who are fully connected to the 'enlightened child' within have no fear of enjoying the pleasure of sex to the maximum and can accept their sexual kinks as needed. It brings such powerful potential to really enjoy not just sex but quite frankly the pleasure of life.

Always with awareness. Bringing the awareness of 'the enlightened child' to one's sexual behaviour often reveals aspects that are really based on trauma being played out again in a sexual format or are reflecting aspects where you disempower yourself in normal life. Often it is good to experiment and let the energy play out. As long as one keeps bringing the awareness of the 'enlightened child' to things over-time these things will find a natural centre and allow the directionless direction of the 'enlightened child' to guide what needs to happen.

It is best to avoid extremes

Like most things on the enlightenment path it is best to avoid extremes. You don't need to be having sex like crazy but perhaps you also don't need to go to the extreme of being celibate either. You don't have to be a saint and totally vanilla but perhaps you also don't have to incorporate all the wild and wonderful things people do in their sex life in the name of 'freedom' and 'experimentation' (often trauma in disguise). People obviously find their own middle ground but very rarely would the directionless direction of the 'enlightened child' result in extreme sexual behaviour, in terms of quantity or type.

The key is being fundamentally honest about your human sexual needs, with no shame, guilt or false spirituality blocking things. This is where many spiritual masters/gurus/teachers who fall prey to sexual scandals fall down. They try to present a bravado to the outside world when behind the scenes they are really hiding things- I would always trust a teacher more who just addressed sex (it is a big human thing so needs to be addressed) in a down to earth and simple way in the context of a broader spiritual and enlightenment picture. It really is that simple and doesn't need to be made into this special thing like Tantra tries to do either. Just have a good honest fuck and get on with life.

Acknowledging the energy exchanged during sex

As we connect more to the 'enlightened child', we also seemingly become more aware of not only our body, thoughts and emotions but also the subtle energy realm. This is very interesting during sex. Most people have sex in an incredibly disconnected way where there is no feeling for the subtle energies that are taking place or how it is affecting each other emotionally- in fact most people try to numb themselves from this completely by always drinking alcohol before sex, taking drugs or just playing it all so safe that there is no room for anything powerful to really come up. The sexual energy is incredibly powerful. When two people are more open spiritually (i.e. more connected to the 'enlightened child' within) there is great potential for the sexual energy to enable a deep transformation in each other. There needs to be a lot of awareness and compassion though. Often shadow sides are revealed when this is the case, which allows great healing and opening to more light within, but can also be very painful and difficult to deal with on a human level.

The first foundation is always a normal approach to sex. Then when you find the right partner who is also connected deeply to the 'enlightened child' this more 'tantric' approach can really start to have some powerful effects. You don't need to do 'tantric practices', you just need to connect to the 'enlightened child' during sex and then stay connected as all the different things happen in the body, thoughts, emotions and subtle energies. It is that simple.

Losing my virginity

For the first twenty two years of my life I was an incredibly supressed person when it came to sexuality. Initially I made a good story about it. I thought it was because I was super pure, spiritual advanced and amazingly disciplined but I soon learnt the truth. The truth was revealed when I first had sex.

I was in what was to be my last year coaching at the University of Exeter, now working as a full-time professional hockey coach having graduated the year before. I decided to go to a local vegan meetup one evening. This was quite an unusual thing for me to do, as although I was a vegan by many years by this point I certainly wasn't a very social able one. It was here I met Kelly. It just had to be a MILF didn't it! Kelly was in her mid- thirties, with a beautiful young daughter who wasn't at the meetup, so she was free to go on the prowl for the night. An innocent young vegan virgin was high on her list. Admittedly I didn't have much competition, as all the other participants there were in their forties and above as Exeter Friends For Animals (who were the hosts of the meeting) hadn't managed to gain any popularity among the younger student population of Exeter. I was quite a novelty at the meeting actually, as they weren't used to young people. After doing the rounds by talking to a wide variety of people at the meeting, I eventually found myself talking to Kelly.

'So where is your young daughter tonight then?' I enquired after we had been talking for ten minutes or so. Admittedly this sounded quite suggestive but I was just trying to be polite. Kelly didn't need much to be led on though. She was wearing tight jeans, with a revealing green top that showed the outline of her pink bra. She has a beautiful refined face, with red pouting lips and a nice tan that didn't seem too fake unless you looked closely.

'Don't worry darling, she is with her Dad for the whole weekend,' she replied, grabbing my thigh under the table as she did so. I tried my best not to react to her movement and play it cool but I was struggling to contain the massive boner that was starting to pierce through my chinos. The meeting was being held on a Friday, so perhaps Kelly was thinking of a sexathon for the whole weekend. I wasn't sure whether I was ready for any sex to be honest. I had never even kissed a Woman before, as the abuse had left me highly traumatised when it came to intimacy, despite my inner convictions that I was really a Buddha in the making.

'Why don't we go for a walk and get out of here?' suggested Kelly, looking me deeply in the eyes with a piercing highly suggestive stare. 'I could do with some company tonight,' she expanded. I nodded my head in agreement, starting to feel my body freezing in parts and the fear coming up from my heart as it suddenly all seemed very real. Was I ready? Was sex a good thing on the spiritual path? Was this in alignment with my highest good? Questions raced through my mind, as we said out goodbyes to the other members of the group and I strode hand in hand with Kelly down the streets of central Exeter.

'Let go straight to yours,' she instructed when we were no more then fifty metres outside of the café where the meeting had been held. I nodded my head in agreement, aware my flat was only two minutes away. I was struggling to speak at this point, as the enormity of what seemed to be happening washed over me and my mind raced with questions.

'I'm going to give you a sexy massage when we get to yours,' shared Kelly in a seductive tone, obviously aware of my inner tension. She pinched my bum, causing me to flinch wildly. 'Oh you like that do you young man,' she enquired tugging her pink bra strap as she did so and playing softly with her wavy blonde hair. I wasn't sure if I liked it or not to be honest- it had just caught me by surprise. I was unsure what to say, so remained silent.

'Oh a silent one are we?' questioned Kelly in a sexy tone. 'I like the silent ones- they are always more mysterious and turn out to be absolute gods in the bedroom.'

I wasn't sure if I was going to be a 'god in the bedroom', considering I was not only a sexual virgin but hadn't even lost my kissing virginity by this point. I was getting more terrified by the minute but breathed deeply and knew on a deeper level that no harm could come to me. I also remained silent.

'Oh you really are playing games with me, you little silent monster,' continued Kelly. 'Your such a bad boy. I'm not sure if you will even get a message when we get in- I might just have to fuck you straight away.'

The boner was only getting more hard in my jeans and there was little time for more thought, as we had arrived at my flat now. I opened the door quickly and instantly made an excuse so could have a minute in the toilet alone. I quickly released the pressure to at least give me a chance of lasting longer than five seconds and made my way back into the lounge to see Kelly.

Kelly was standing there full prepared. She had taken off her tight blue jeans and green top to reveal a beautiful set of pink lingerie- the pink thong exposed her sexy bottom very well and her bra really brought out her large breasts. She looked at me with a mischievous grin. I imagine being a Mum brought lots of pressure and restraint into her life, so this was an opportunity to let go and enjoy different sides of herself.

'Strip naked for me beautiful,' she instructed in a firm tone. I didn't want to disappoint this beautiful Woman, so quickly whipped my clothes off and stood there waiting for the next instruction. My boner had quickly come back again. 'Well show me where the bedroom is then darling,' she said, laughing as she did so at my incompetence and lack of forwardness. 'You haven't done this before have you?' she asked, which made me blush as I nodded to confirm she was right in her assumption of my sexual novice status.

'This way,' I said, my arm starting to shake as fear went through my body and panic started to come up. Would I be safe with her? Could I trust her? Oh my God what if she raped me? Crazy intrusive thoughts rushed through my mind, which I couldn't control. I had started to disassociate from my body and it was like I was watching a movie on the screen rather than actually participating in the action.

She got me to lie front on the bed, trying to relax me as much as possible for a sexy massage. I buried my head in the covers of the bed and tried my best not to think about things. She gently started to brush my back, which helped me relax. She then proceeded to massage my aching legs (I had been on a run earlier in the day) and also started to gently caress my feet. Despite occasionally flinching this felt much better and I was starting to feel more comfortable about things- perhaps this whole sex thing was ok after all.

'Right spread your legs nice and wide dear. I want to explore that lovely bottom of yours,' she instructed. I wasn't exactly sure what she intended on doing (maybe she just wanted to massage it properly) but I followed her instructions like the good virgin I was. Kelly whipped off her bra and her knickers quickly, then started to moan as she started to play with her own body. I wasn't exactly sure what she was doing, as my face was still facing the bed, but the moans gave me a good idea.

'Oh you have been a very naughty boy haven't you Jack?' she questioned in a rhetorical manner. 'You need to be licked out very deeply, you naughty little boy.' She proceeded to go onto all fours, before launching herself at my bottom with her tongue. I flinched wildly as her tongue made contact with my arsehole. I hadn't been expecting that! My legs kicked out wide and my upper body shivered on the bed but Kelly was persistent, pinning me down with her two hands and licking me ferociously. Part of me felt like I was being raped, part of me was very confused with what was happening and part of me was enjoying the pleasure of it. I started to disassociate very strongly again, as the pain of the supressed trauma became too much and I allowed her to do whatever she wanted to my body. I was hers to use how she wanted.

The next couple of hours passed by, with me in this sort of transcendental state where I was more of an observer than an active participant in the sex I had with Kelly. After thoroughly rimming me, she proceeded to get out a condom and then ride me in cow-girl for pretty much the entirety of our time together. Perhaps she thought that I was some sort of tantric master. I managed to maintain my erection the whole time without ejaculating and she seemed to get a huge amount of pleasure from the process. I was in a transcendental state of shock the whole time, half feeling like I was being raped and half feeling as though I was watching a pre-destined divine movie playing out on the screen. Eventually Kelly had received enough pleasure and stopped. We cuddled for a while before she said her good-byes and said she would call me the next morning to check in with how I was and arrange the next time we could see each other.

When she did call I had to be honest with her- I wasn't ready to have any more sex, let alone a proper relationship which it seemed was what she really wanted. I was no longer a virgin but I was still a highly traumatised human being who had received an enlightenment experience.

Visiting a Tantric Goddess

After the shallowing experience with Kelly I decided to abstain from sex for the next two years. I tried to do lots of work with it on the various people I worked with, looking at the fears, emotions, thoughts and energies that were keeping the trauma in place. It was helping but something just didn't quite feel right. I eventually figured out that I really needed to work on the body aspect of it, which made me decide to look into tantric massage. This sometimes had a bad name. It made you imagine a naughty man in his mid fifties seeking some excitement outside of his dull marriage and fidget wife but it was really an ancient practice that used the sexual energy to help someone transform. It sounded like the perfect thing to help me with my sexual trauma.

I had booked in a series of sessions with a tantric goddess to help me achieve sexual embodiment and confidence. The lady was in her mid forties and called Kiara. She had sounded really nice, if a little mysterious down the phone, as we agreed the overall focus for my six sessions and the focus of the first session. Each session was to be three hours long. The first session would be an introductory session, focusing on some emotional release, some counselling, some breathing practices and then my first ever tantric massage.

On the day of our first session, I was feeling excited yet also a little nervous. She had given me the address for her 'temple' in Stroud, which seemed to be in a residential area but maybe the map on the internet wasn't quite accurate. I tried to stay as centred and focused as possible during the hour long drive there. After going down the motorway, I eventually turned off into a small village and stopped outside a series of terraced residential areas. The internet had been right. The 'temple' actually turned out to be a small two bed dirty looking terraced house in a run down area of a village, which made me feel a little uneasy but I was also realistic that Kiara probably wasn't raking it in from the tantric work.

I nervously got out of my car, breathing deeply. I walked up to the 'temple' and rang the doorbell, eager to see what Kiara looked like in person and praying that I fancied her enough to want her to touch my body but not so much that I would ejaculate in five seconds. She opened the door. Liker her photos she was an attractive but not stunning Woman in her mid forties, with wavy brown hair, a curvy figure, average sized breasts and a nice warm inviting smile. She fitted the bill just perfectly I thought.

'You must be Jack?' she enquired, offering me a hug. She was wearing a white priestess outfit, which really brought out her curves and had also made the effort to apply some make-up. It was classy above anything else. 'Please do take a seat in the chamber of truth,' she instructed me, pointing towards what looked like a lounge but like everything in this 'temple' seemed to have mysterious and magical names. It sounded like something out of Harry Potter.

'Right I want you to close your eyes as we begin and we will do a meditation to help you connect to the energies of the temple,' she instructed, before proceeding to take me through a twenty minutes meditation that in all fairness was rather good. After setting some clearly worded intentions for the session, we moved onto some clearing exercises. I had to beat up an innocent pillow to let unhealed anger out of my system, scream and shout at a cardboard face that I imagined was both my parents and other people I had issues with and then finally I had to dance around like a mad-man to give any final trapped emotions a chance to break free. Some good strong emotions came up for clearing. Kiara seemed pleased with my progress and we settled down for the counselling part of the session before the main event of the tantric massage.

'Yes I feel like I still hold a lot of trauma from the abuse that happened,' I confided in Kiara, who was staring intensely at me and making some notes.

'Yes this is good, tell me more about it Jack and I will tune in,' she said, dropping her pen and starting to breath deeply as she 'tuned in' to her intuition.

'Well I have all these powerful emotions came up during sex that make me very scared. The abuse destroyed my confidence you see. It is like I am playing out the trauma again and again and can't break free of it. It hurts to be honest and I just want to be normal,' I shared in a vulnerable manner. I could feel Kiara tense up at this point and a new harder side of her seemed to emerge from the previously compassionate priestess.

'Well all this trauma is just your story Jack. It is just a story,' she repeated in a manner which felt a little disconnected and almost like an accusation. Sure we could say from the perspective of the 'enlightened child' that every aspect of our humanity is a story but I always felt it was best to be honest and confront the very human side of things too. It was almost like she had swallowed a non-duality textbook and was just repeating a phrase that was disconnected from the heart energy of the moment. After this I felt much more uncomfortable in our conversation and unwilling to share much more but we managed to keep it going for the next twenty minutes or so.

83

'Right lets go to the chamber of pleasure,' she instructed, which turned out to be a small bedroom with a mattress in the middle of it. She left me alone in the room for a minute or so, as she collected some things from another room to help us with our tantric massage. I contemplated the journey I had made so far. It was like my whole sexual history flashed before my eyes, as I saw the trauma in childhood, the many times I had held back from welcoming females in my teenage years and the night I lost my virginity with Kelly. I was feeling very nervous but also excited that I had the courage to go into the unknown. These things only ever helped in my experience. Eventually Kiara returned to the room, with some condoms, lube, massage oil and one or two other things that I didn't recognise. She nervously made her way over to me, looking me deeply in the eyes. I'm not sure if she was trying to be sexy but I felt quite awkward to be honest and a little unsure what was going to happen next.

'Right let's start with the clothing ritual,' Kiara instructed from her position at the end of the mattress alongside me.

'What's that then?' I questioned, trying to keep it cool as much as possible and avoid coming across too nervous.

'A ritual to help you set the intention for what you are going to let go of in a divine encounter,' she replied in a rather unnecessarily grand manner. 'We are going to sit opposite each other, lovingly looking into each other's eyes from only a couple of metres away. Then we are going to remove one piece of clothing at a time. Each time we do this we will set an intention for what we want to let go of in our divine encounter, slowly building the combined energy between us. Are you happy with all of this Jack?' she enquired. I nodded my head in agreement and tried to work out what I wanted to let go of.

'Right I will start,' she said in an upbeat tone. Obviously she was keen to whip of her priestess dress and get right down to her panties right away. 'I let go of my inhibitions around young men,' she exclaimed in a seductive manner, looking at me deeply in the eyes and reminding me more of Kelly by the second. Off came her white priestess dress to reveal a beautifully seductive red bra and thong, which seemed slightly inappropriate to the divine intentions of tantra. In all fairness she had explained in the initial call that she would wear something as sexy as possible to help get my sexual energy flowing, which she felt was important given my history. We had also agreed clear boundaries and safe communication for every action. This was very different from my random evening with Kelly, which had brought up much rape trauma. I felt in control and totally clear on what we were doing, if momentarily a little surprised by the choice of exercise.

'I let go of my inability to receive pleasure,' I shared in a more downbeat tone, starting to feel my body (more specifically the region around my genital area) starting freeze up and fear coming up very strongly in my heart. I took off my blue Jack Wills jumper, which didn't exactly have the same impact as Kiara's initial move but one must play by the rules of the game. By the time Kiara was fully naked, I was still in my chinos but we ploughed on regardless and eventually I was left with just my boxer shorts on.

'I let go of my inability to receive a Women's love,' I boldly stated, getting much more into the flow and whipping off my Calvin Klein boxer shorts that were hiding my already full erect penis. Breath Jack, breath I kept reminding myself. It wouldn't exactly be the most tantric thing in the world if I ejaculated without Kiara even touching me, especially since Tantra was supposed to be all about maintaining the male life force energy and not ejaculating.

'Right if you just life down on the mattress love,' instructed Kiara in a gentle tone (momentarily forgetting the divine naming of things), as we finished gazing into each other's eyes and both did our best to ignore the animal urge to check out other parts of the body. I lay down on my back, secretly hoping she might go straight into the Lingham massage.

'No Jack, if you just lie on your front first love. We are going to honour the back of your body first,' she shared in a soothing tone. I wasn't sure if the back of my body needed honouring but I was happy to go with the flow.

Kiara took a deep breath in and then walked over to the windowsill where she had placed the massage oil. She then gently knelt beside me and started to apply the oil. She had lit some candles in the room and had also turned on some relaxing music, which was playing very quietly in the background. I tried to stop any disassociation from my body, breathing deeply into any pain that arose and trying to trust the process of what was unfolding. It seemed to work. I started to relax more deeply than I ever had in my body, as she gently massaged me all over the back in a way that seemed to open up energy channels I never knew existed. I was almost in a trance state. This was very different from the disassociation I had experienced with Kelly though, as it was a grounded trance state where the transcendence was experienced through the vessel of the body rather than above it. This was proving to be a good decision I thought to myself. I'm not sure how much I had got out of the previous couple of hours but this last hour for tantric massage was certainly hitting all the right notes.

'If you just turn onto your front my dear,' instructed Kiara in a gentle tone. I momentarily got out of the body-accessed tranced state I was in and turned over. This felt like the business end of things now. I half motioned towards my penis in a confident manner, with this boldness seemingly coming out of me from nowhere. Perhaps I was too conditioned from the intense sexual experience with Kelly and was forgetting this was a mystical process of Tantra.

'We are not quite ready for the lingam massage yet,' replied Kiara to my non-verbal gesture. This was the first time I wasn't restricted to having my eyes having to look at hers in the clothing ritual or facing down onto the mattress. Inevitably the inner human took over in me and I had a little glance at her nice set of breasts, as well as a cheeky look at her vagina out of the corner of my eye.

'If you just lie on your back Jack,' continued Kiara, trying her best to ignore my wondering eyes. We both knew though. 'I am going to just relax the front of your body first and then we will move onto the lingam massage, where we will try to help you have the best orgasm of your life.'

That sounded like a plan to me! I tried my best to relax, as she massaged the front of my body with her beautiful hand and the luscious oil. It was much harder though. Even though I closed my eyes again and tried my best to focus on my breathing, the fact that her hand was relatively close to my penis kept me very aroused and seemingly on the brink of ejaculating any minute. I was learning how to control 'little Prefontaine' though. The key seemed to be breathing very deeply and allowing the sexual energy to circulate around the body, rather than splosh it out all in one go. Eventually the moment came.

'Right lets move onto the lingam massage,' she shared, as 'little Prefontaine' celebrated in the background. There was one clear issue with getting what was basically a fancy hand job from a stranger though.

'I just need to get a condom out and also get some gloves for my hands before we do it,' shared Kiara, smashing any sense of sexuality that was in the air and replacing it with a feeling that I was a laboratory animal in an experiment. At least I was still getting a hand job though- wasn't all bad!

'Right I just need to explain the orgasm process for you,' shared Kiara, once she had placed her gloves on and the condom on 'little Prefontaine'. She went on to explain the breathing process I should follow to get the maximum amount of pleasure flowing and how it needed to interact with the movements she would break. I had never realised having an orgasm was so complicated!

Eventually her white gloved hand slid down to 'little Prefontaine'. She stroked me up and down slowly, using what seemed to be some sort of magical technique that certainly wasn't used in porn movies. I felt good and relaxed, though I wasn't convinced I was about to have an orgasm. Kiara seemed to be doing everything she could to invoke it though.

'Look at me in the eyes,' she instructed in a firm manner, which I did immediately. 'Now bring that energy up Jack, deep breaths deep breaths, up and up to that crown chakra.'

I was trying my best but I wasn't sure it was working- I had managed to focus enough not to ejaculate but I didn't feel like I was about to have a mind blowing orgasm anytime soon.

'Ahhh, ohhhh, yessss,' she screamed, seemingly getting an orgasm from giving me the advanced hand job. She looked me deeply in the eyes, as she continued to make powerful sexual noises. There was only one way to respond.

'Ahhhhh, yessss, ohhhhh Kiara,' I screamed, doing the best fake orgasm impression I could muster. I had never expected my first orgasm to occur this way. I had imagined a deeply tantric and sensual experience with the love of my life but the reality turned out to be a fake orgasm with a middle aged Woman giving me a posh hand job in a dirty terraced house in the middle of an isolated town in the Cotswolds. I suppose not everything works out as you dreamed.

An unexpected pleasure adventure

After doing some more work with Kiara, I continued my little pleasure adventure with more tantric massages off various people. I was a rather good recipient by the end of my little experiment. It seemed to significantly help me get much more comfortable with my sexual energy and being in my body during intimacy but I knew that I needed to go to the next level. I had made a radical spiritual conclusion by this point. All the work with spiritual masters and various modalities could only take me so far in healing from the abuse- what was actually going to be more effective now was sleeping with Women. Perhaps my high performance sports coaching background was helpful. It didn't take a spiritual genius to work out that the best way to get more comfortable with sex and physical intimacy was to practise it a lot- perhaps I had needed to do all the previous spiritual work followed by the tantric bodywork to get to this point, to enable the harsher aspects of the trauma to be dealt with and also be completely comfortable in dealing with it when it reared its ugly head now and again during sex.

As a next step I initiated the tinder experiment. Using the tinder dating app I would go on a little adventure the next year and a half, building my confidence up massively with sex and making up for all that lost ground as a teenager and Uni student. I was a man on a mission. There was much intelligence and fun with what happened next, as I got to gradually build up my confidence and practical experience with a wide variety of women. It was lucky I didn't consider myself very spiritual by this point, as it wasn't the most traditional spiritual look. I was always very respectful and honest with the Women I met on tinder, which seemed to amaze many of them. I was equally amazed at how many single Women just wanted sex and nothing more, which suited me perfectly at this point. And some outrageous things happened.

I had been very lucky to have met Orla, a beautiful local Portuguese women in her mid thirties. She was a reiki master, a masseur and most importantly wasn't looking for any serious commitment having only recently completed a divorce. This suited me just perfectly for that moment in time. We had slept together a few times and had developed a nice rapport, which had led her to offer me a tantric massage (which she had been trained in). I played innocent. Rather than share it was déjà vu all over again, I played it cool and pretended I had never received a tantric massage before.

In all fairness I had never received a tantric massage as good at the one Orla gave me. Oh my God it was heaven. I think the fact that we actually had a genuine connection made it all the more luscious, as well as the fact that she was super hot and very good with her hands. No point in making it too mystical! Although things were about to get more mystical and crazy about an hour into my first tantric massage with her...

'Do you mind if we get some other ladies involved?' she whispered seductively into my ear, as she was doing this amazing body to body massage technique I had never experienced before. I immediately opened my eyes in shock.

'What?' I questioned, just ensuring I had heard her right.

'Well I sometimes like to play with more than just one person and explore my bi-sexual side too. I have a couple of friends visiting from Portugal and I thought you would be keen to get involved, so they are already ready for you.'

One can only decide to go with the flow or not in these sort of crazy moments. I decided to flow.

'Great,' shared Orla. 'I will just go and get them from the other room.'. She proceeded to walk out of the door naked, instructing me to stay still on the bed, as she went into the other bedroom. I had been so fixated on getting her into bed the moment I walked into the door that I could have easily missed a couple of strangers being in the house.

'You must be Jack,' said an extremely attractive lady with dyed blonde hair and long legs, who also looked like she was in her mid-thirties. She was followed by a much smaller Women with black hair and large breasts. All had the traditional Mediterranean tan and had the normal gorgeous Latino behind.

It feels unnecessary to share the details of what happened after that but it would be fair to say it was a memorable sexual experience. I was certainly getting more and more confident to the point that I was ready to have a girlfriend. Intimate relationships had always been challenging for me.

Chapter 7-
Enlightenment and
Relationships

Relationships are such a key part of life. Above anything else connecting to the 'enlightened child' helps you become much more aware of all the bodily sensations, thoughts, emotions and subtle energies that are being played out in relationships. This is often very helpful. It brings much more understanding to what is truly happening in a relationship, allowing greater compassion to oneself and more importantly greater compassion to the other person too. Nowhere is this more important than intimate relationships.

Surely the greatest challenge of life has to be intimate relationships? Fuck all the search for enlightenment, the search for mystic spiritual gifts and the search for the ultimate philosophy- if two people could generally dance together in a functional intimate relationship that was balanced and empowered both parties then that would certainly something to celebrate.

<u>Seeing the limitations of one human being</u>
Perhaps there is no bigger block to love than our obsession (sometimes overt but often subtle) with the belief that one person is suddenly going to solve all our need for love and other needs we have. We invest far too much hope in 'the one' in my opinion. Now I would still like to keep the magic alive and a little hope but also taint it with the realism of the human condition. Enlightenment reveals many things. One of the biggest things is that we are all fucked up human beings, who have a wide range of needs, desires and wants. These appear to disappear when one sits deeply in the 'enlightened child' but will always remain when one is in a human body. The advantage of a re-connection to the 'enlightened child' is that you can see your needs and particular quirks far more clearly, as well as accurately assess

them in others to a much higher level. This is very powerful when it comes to intimate relationships.

Firstly it completely destroys this notion that one person can meet all my needs for love, which is absolutely ridiculous when you see through the illusion of it. That is not to advise polyamory (which is nearly always rooted in the avoidance of hurt) but instead helps you see clearly the importance of friends, family and aligned career work that meets other needs for love and reduces the pressure on 'the one'. It simplifies things. It helps you see the basic human needs that you really require from a relationship (often pleasurable sex, a certain level of income, a certain societal reputation, a certain age, a certain look and more basic things), more emotionally intimate needs you can't get from elsewhere (being vulnerable, sharing your deepest fears/secrets, getting a deep support with your goals etc), a healthy dose of what we call love (in a way which can't be gained from others and often overlaps with basic physical intimacy needs and emotional intimacy needs) and then this mystical magical thing called 'spark'. The hardest thing to assess, even with advanced awareness, and one that requires careful consideration.

Does the 'spark' come from the 'enlightened child' or heavy karma?

Nearly all of us have been in the position where we feel a 'spark' with a new person. Some of the more sexually charged or maybe lucky of us feel 'spark' with lots of people, whilst for others it happens much more infrequently. 'Spark' is a dangerous thing. It often causes us to drop lots of our very real needs and just following the feeling into the inevitable sex and physical connection. There is nothing wrong with this. It just often leads to a lot of heartbreak, pain and trouble further down the line as we realise the incompatibility of the person we are now in a relationship with, once the initial 'spark' has faded somewhat.

In my experience working with clients 'spark' can come in one of two forms- it either comes from the 'spark' of unresolved karma or from the 'spark' of the 'enlightened child'. It is good to have fun with both sparks. When the 'spark' comes from unresolved karma the fleshliness of the sexual attraction tends to be stronger, the wild emotions tend to be stirred more and the practicalities of being in a relationship with the other person tend to be much more flaky. In short it tends to be the perfect setting for an intense short-term union that blows up. In contrast 'spark' that comes from the 'enlightened child' tends to have a softer yet deeper sexual attraction, emotions that are more consistent with peace and the practicalities of being in a relationship with the other person tend be more far more solid. In short it tends to be perfect for a longer-term union that leads to mutual growth for both parties. They won't necessarily be 'the one' but they certainly help move you along your spiritual path more than the unresolved karma ones.

With the karma ones it is good to experiment and play some out sexually to start. Then over-time once your awareness gets better, there is much value in being able to feel the energy and let it resolve itself naturally without resorting to playing out sexual intimacy to do it. This tends to lead to much more peace and less relationship drama.

Being able to be alone when single or alone when in a relationship is a valuable life skill

A deeper connection to the 'enlightened child' certainly lends itself to being better at being able to be alone. There is much value in this when it comes to intimate relationships. It is quite frankly impossible to love another human being, without first having discovered a sense of love for yourself in your own aloneness. So it helps with being more loving. It also has immense practical benefit in enabling you to make empowered decisions when it comes to your intimate relationships, as you don't make decisions from a fearful place of being alone. You only decide to enter an intimate relationship if it adds real value to your life. So many of us enter or stay in intimate relationships because we are scared to be truly alone and face our own shadow in this place. This really stops our spiritual growth (i.e. connection to 'the enlightened child' growth). My theory is that this connection to the 'enlightened child' tends to grow fastest when we have enough alone time in a single life (relationships require a lot of energy) but that we grow fastest on a human level when we are in relationships (bar disempowered relationships that drag on for years in the same pattern again and again). So perhaps the ideal is this- a deep exploration of the 'enlightened child' at dedicated points in your life when you are single combined with a deep joy and fun at all the wonderful human things a fulfilling intimate relationship brings when you are in one. That way we grow spiritually and as a human being too!

Another factor is this unhealthy obsession most of us have with always being in contact with the person we are in an intimate relationship with. I always feel more space is better. The vast majority of people's intimate relationships are co-dependent, which lends itself to this illusion that a healthy intimate relationship requires contact everyday and a huge amount of time together. A deeper connection to the aloneness of the 'enlightened child' destroys this illusion. Although evidently we would all want a consistency and decent amounts of contact in our intimate relationships, I don't see any harm in not being in contact at set periods during the year and each person being happy doing their own thing. Having space to breath outside of a relationship is so vital. It allows more time and space for the other relationships in our life that love and nurture us in different ways, as well as more appreciation of the other person when we do connect with them. Less is often more, as the old saying goes!

Intimate relationships hurt but nothing can ever really go wrong at a deeper level

If there is one thing in life that will stir your bodily sensations, thoughts, emotions and subtle energies it is when intimate relationship go wrong. Someone cheating on you, a divorce, a lie or a falling out of love with a person you once held in such high regard all hurt at a deep level. Yet there is some consolation. There is no doubt that in the human domain of our existence a lot can and does go wrong in intimate relationships, which results in so much pain, hurt and regret for all involved. This is just the human drama though. At a deeper level when viewed purely from the space of the 'enlightened child', nothing can truly ever go wrong and all is unfolding just as it is meant too. Perhaps if you have just experienced some extreme hurt that isn't much consolation currently! Yet over-time or now this instant what it does open you up to is the deeper truth that everyone is eternally innocent- you can forgive your deepest mistakes in relationships and also forgive other's mistakes that you have been on the receiving end of. All is still radiantly peaceful in the 'enlightened child'.

Balancing each other out

Perhaps the 'ultimate' intimate relationships are one where there is a deeper connection through the 'enlightened child' in you both but on a human level you balance each other out well. I have always found myself telling clients who want help with their intimate relationships that it was best to seek someone 'different from them'. This needs a careful explanation. Obviously there needs to be enough shared values, shared ability to fit into each other's life stages and a shared sexual connection as a basis, as well as a mysterious spark from the 'enlightened child'. Yet outside of that difference should be valued. Different interests, different personalities and different ways of reacting to things bring much richness and learning to each other's lives in a way that someone who was more similar to you never would. It also leads to far more fun and humour. Nothing is more soul destroying than a serious intimate relationship with two serious people. In contrast having quite stark differences with two people with a sense of humour brings much fun and laughter, in a way that opens the soul to deeper and deeper levels of love. Appreciate differences and your intimate relationships are likely to thrive.

The illusion of the twin flame or soul mate

Perhaps there is no deeper spiritual illusion than the concept of the twin flame or soul mate- especially the twin flame, like vom! We have already touched on these briefly in the chapter on spirituality. Now we will look at them much more closely, destroying the illusion once and for all to the point that we can accept that we are just a normal human being looking for this magical mysterious thing called love. I believed in twin flames and soul mates for a period. I have already shared lots of 'embarrassing' and funny stories in this book from my spiritual journey but nothing is as cringeworthy and hilarious as my experience with a women who I thought was my twin flame.

Firstly for the spiritual novices amongst us we need to be clear on the difference between twin flames and soul mates. You see spiritual people love specialness. And there is nothing more special than an intimate relationship in the human experience, so the specialness gets ramped up in intensity when it gets projected onto intimate relationships. With quite hilarious results, as you will see. According to the quite illogical spiritual logic there is a distinct difference between twin flames and soul mates. Apparently twin flames are two halves of the whole, where soul mates are not. While twin flames are thought to be one soul split into two bodies, soul mates are simply two separate souls that are extraordinarily linked together. This has some huge spiritual consequences in terms of the purpose of the respective relationships apparently. The higher purpose of a soul mate relationship is the growth and evolution of one's own consciousness, whereas the higher purpose for twin flames is creating a higher vibration and consciousness for the entire planet through ascending together with your combined energy.

No pressure then!

When you combine the need for most spiritual people to have some sort of grand purpose and also a massive specialness in the difference of their intimate relationships to the rest of humanity, you can start to get a good idea where the whole twin flame and soul mate concept comes from. I would prefer to take a more grounded and honest approach.

Lets firstly look at soul mates. Although it is certainly true we feel more connected to certain human beings than others and maybe even feel particularly connected to one person, soul mates have some underlying assumptions in them that I feel don't help. Firstly too much focus on the soul and not enough on the human being. Subtly the whole soulmate concept tends to make you focus on the soul connection above anything else, which can be easily used as spiritual escapism to deny and not address the very real human aspect of it. As you open up you can feel connected too many souls but it doesn't always mean the human elements of it are ideal. Secondly this obsessive focus on using relationships to grow and evolve one's own consciousness can only cause ugliness- how can one possibly love when the focus is on growing oneself through a relationship? The growth happens naturally. It is much better to simply focus on enjoying all the beautiful things an intimate relationship brings into your life and accepting the other person exactly how they are (in their light, good, bad and darkness), rather than merely using them as on object for your own spiritual growth in some grand manner.

Then we move onto twin flames. This quite possibly has to be the most ugly yet also the most hilarious concept in the history of humanity. Oh how much fun you can have with twin flames and all those idiots offering 'twin flame coaching'. Before we delve into the destruction of the twin flame concept (in a peaceful manner I might add remembering I am supposed to have had an enlightenment experience and all that), we should also briefly touch on the 'twin flames stages'. This is again illogical spiritual logic that there are certain set phases to the twin flame relationship, which differ slightly from idiot to idiot but generally look something like this…

Stage 1- Seeking the one
Stage 2- Glimpsing the one
Stage 3- Falling in love
Stage 4- Inner purging (soul growth)
Stage 5- The runner and the chaser
Stage 6- Surrender
Stage 7- Reunion/Joining

Apparently the twin flame journey story goes something like this (fasten your spiritual seatbelts by the way, as it is one hell of a tale). You first start to seek the one. You then are lucky enough to catch a glimpse of them (perhaps after a number of 'fake twins' who you initially think are your twin flame but turn out not to be). You then madly fall in love and it is a love not of this world that you have never experienced before. Initially it is all fairy tales but then both your shadow sides come up, with all your issues, past pain and trauma from previous relationships and other aspects of your life. This leads to the end of the relationship. You are still very energetically connected though, which leads to problems. You enter the 'runner and chaser' phase where one of you chases the relationship whilst the other one runs away from it (you can also alternate between being the runner and chaser). Over-time as you mature spiritually you both start to surrender to the process and are ready to join with your twin flame. The fairy tale then recommences as you join with your twin flame and come together to do your mission for the world.

What a load of total bollocks!

When peacefully destroying the twin flame concept we first need to consider the whole concept about what twin flames are. It reveals a lot. As human beings disconnected from the 'enlightened child' we consistently feel like something is missing from our lives, which we then project outwards onto other people, achievements and status symbols. Nowhere is this more clear than in the twin flame concept. Here the other person is not merely their own independent human being but is quite literally the 'other half' of my own soul. It is what has always been missing from me. Some clever twin flame people try to sneakily get around this problem. They claim the twin flame journey is a mirror for the evolution of my own consciousness and just a trigger for changes within- although certainly things that appear to be outside of us can be helpful I am not convinced that one person can really have such a profound impact on our life. It also creates a clear delusion. You play along with the whole inner game to sound more advanced spiritually and like you know the real deeper truth behind things but still actually believe in the twin flame concept, with all the stages and idea of it being the other half of your own soul. It is just a silly lie. Those who see past the whole twin flame concept can see intimate relationships for what they are- no spiritual concept, just two human beings trying to do their best with things and hopefully having some fun along the way too.

Next in our peaceful destruction we can start to look at the stages one by one. It seems a little rogue that the first stage is starting to seek 'the one'. I mean don't like 99.9% of human beings do that on some level? The vast majority just don't make it a whole concept around twin flames because they are atheists/religious and not spiritual. The second stage is where the real delusion starts. It is actually quite sad to go onto twin flames groups and see people's utter conviction that they really have found their 'twin flame'. Perhaps what is even sadder is when you see people in relationships who completely believe they have completed the 'twin flame journey' and are now doing their mission with their twin flame. Particularly if it is actually quite a disempowering relationship. Stages three and four (falling in love, followed by the inner purging) are really true for any relationships we encounter. Processing happens, especially within the heart opening power of an intimate relationship and also when we start to connect to the 'enlightened child' more (whether we define that as being spiritual or not). The fifth stage (the runner and the chaser) is perhaps when the most comedy comes into the proceedings. I have literally had clients convinced they have found their twin flame but they are in the 'runner/chaser' phase until I gently point out that the fact their 'twin flame' is in another country and with another person makes it quite unlikely they will get into a relationship with you. It is often just a karmic relationship processing, with nothing ever meant to happen on a physical level in this lifetime. The runner and chaser phased is basically a pseudonym for justifying why that bastard who is your twin flame doesn't want to be in a relationship with you when you act like a big spiritual weirdo and are completely incompatible on every level. My twin flame was a bastard too and a very fast runner. Despite me doing everything I could, she kept running away from me again and again as you will see in the story below. She never came back unfortunately but luckily I had given up the twin flame concept by then. The final stages of surrender and dissolution are basically a steal from common wisdom around enlightenment and this grand surrender into the dissolution of 'all that is'. It is like a double piece of absolute bollocks. A stupid concept to make enlightenment seem this great mystery and this grand mergence with the universe process (for fuck sake there is no universe or nothing outside of you) but also an even stupider concept when brought into the already stupid twin flame concept. Stupid shenanigans all round.

My twin flame kept running away from me

Finally I had found my twin flame! After pining for at least a couple of years for the one, finally she had appeared. Maybe I should have been expecting it after all the 11:11 symbols I had been seeing but still love takes you by surprise hey. And it was flowing well. We weren't quite shagging each other from the rooftops yet or changing the world but we were at least planning to work together on a big yoga project for our generation. Destiny was unfolding right before my eyes.

Everything seemed to be fitting together perfectly. She was about four years younger than me, had been born in another country and in terms of character was in many ways my opposite. This fitted well with how twin flames normally were. They tended to come from different backgrounds apparently and also were your opposites in terms of personality, so they could trigger your shadow side. There certainly was a lot of tension between us but it seemed healthy enough to me. Then there was the energy. A mysterious connection was present, which meant I could feel her thoughts, emotions and feelings even when we weren't together, as well as almost feel her physical presence when I went to sleep at night. It was intense but again all seemed to align with the normal story of a twin flame journey.

After things going well for a period, disaster struck. She had decided she didn't want to work on the yoga project any more. Luckily because of my understanding of the twin flame journey, I wasn't too concerned and understood it was just the stage five runner and chaser phase. We had already fallen in love in my eyes (though there had been no physical relationship) and had definitely been through some inner purging through our connection. Despite my experience with all things twin flame, my heart was still broken and I couldn't help but become a chaser. I offered her all my yoga equipment for free (which she accepted), my video camera to help her with her work on the yoga project (which she accepted), gave her a beautiful pink necklace (which she also accepted) and sent her a lovely card with an apology for saying I had hurt her feelings. I then waited. In my mind I was now entering stage six of surrender and it would only be a matter of time before we would be together. Months passed by. Nothing was bloody happening! So I emailed her requesting an in-person meeting to discuss our connection but she refused. I tried a couple of times more over the next few months but she kept saying no and running away. She really was also running far, as in her last message she shared she was moving back to Australia to be with her extended family. Things weren't looking good.

Eventually I realised we weren't twin flames and through more enlightening experiences really saw past the whole twin flame illusion. I could instead just be a normal human being with normal relationship needs- very refreshing! Something was still slightly bothering me though. Not only had my twin flame ran away from me, she had also ended up with nearly a thousand pounds worth of my goods. Bloody twin flames! Not only do they break your heart, though also destroy your bank balance too.

A note on parents

Perhaps there is no relationship more challenging than the one with our parents. They always say parents are the greatest mirror to ourselves. When viewed from the space of the 'enlightened child' we can see very clearly that our parents are perfectly innocent and were just trying their best with the limited capacity of being human that they had at their disposal. All was fine at a deeper level. When viewed from the space of the human being (body, thoughts, emotions, subtle energies) we can see very clearly that as well as having many strengths, our parents also have weaknesses too. It is called being human.

The big breakthrough is when we see parents were trying their best...love then emerges. They certainly may have many faults, have harmed us in many ways and been quite insufficient as parents on many levels but with their limited human faculties they still tried their best. Even if it didn't seem like it.

A note on extended family and friends

Got to be honest I never got the whole 'extended family' vibe-I much preferred my friends, as I had free will over who to choose then and don't have to fake it to make it.

When it comes to friends the best ones on an enlightenment path are always the unspiritual ones...they often turn out to be more spiritual in the long-run anyway. Friends need to meet your human needs. These are so varied and different from person to person it is quite impossible to give any advice, other than stressing the importance of focusing on normal grounded friends who align with your human needs. It is that simple really! Don't be one of those dickheads who only as 'spiritual friends' or friends of a 'high vibration'- those people are nearly always in spiritual denial and scared of life.

Also I personally love having friends of different ages and from no groups. I have a very good friend who is sixty-five, as well as friends who are middle-aged Women and friends my own age- I am one weird bloke to be honest but it flows for me. One distinction is I have zero friends from a set group. I have absolutely no idea whether this has anything to do with the enlightenment experience or not but I prefer to walk alone- not in a way where I make myself an island (I have lots of friends) but in a way where I am not too tied to the consciousness/patterns/social requirements of any one group. I catch up individually with friends and that works for me.

Chapter 8-
Enlightenment and Healing

<u>The 'enlightened child' changes it all</u>
There are many different layers to healing but the connection to and understanding of the 'enlightened child' completely changes the whole paradigm when it comes to healing. All of medicine and alternative healing is in the 'human realm' (i.e. the body, thoughts, emotions and subtle energies). This includes traditional medicine, psychology, psychotherapy, inner child healing, energy healing, nutrition, massage, physiotherapy, channelling and many other modalities. Pretty much everything is valid and can be helpful in certain ways. Never listen to the idiots who try to completely disregard traditional medicine or idiots who aren't open to more esoteric things such as energy healing. Just find what works for you and flow with it, always being open to change and improvement.

All of these things in the 'human realm' are reliant on time, evolution and progress. There appears to be a movement from the past to the present and from the present to the future. In addition there is also often logic to it or at least some sort of understanding with what appears to be happening. In contrast the 'enlightened child' is not reliant on time, evolution or progress, with it just being what it is (there is no movement in time because it is outside of time and space). In addition there is no logic to it because it is outside of the human mind and completely beyond human understanding (but alas we try with books like this). It is in the 'enlightened child' that miracles can appear to happen. Things can completely change in an instant for a person because it is not reliant on the normal human constraints that limit the speed of progress and the normal laws of the human condition simply don't apply.

It is a little tricky to sometimes see or understand what has happened though because we are very plugged into the human condition and don't really see cause and effect clearly at all. For example someone connected to the 'enlightened child' could initiate a huge change in a person just through a normal conversation without anything grand taking place on a worldly level, even though the deeper soul programme and limitations blocking their progress has completely changed. Things will then unfold in a completely different way for that person but they would never ever be able to connect it back to that conversation.

The second key difference with the 'enlightened child' compared to the human realm is that in the 'enlightened child' everything is already healed. It is this property that allows the miracle to take place. In the 'enlightened child' because there is no time and it isn't really in the human condition, there is no illness, no sickness and nothing can ever be wrong. All is fine. By connecting to the 'enlightened child' through the vessel of one's humanity miracles can then take place, as the 'enlightened child' collapses time and the constraints of what appears to be possible. It is here that things can get tricky. It is perfectly legitimate to say that the 'enlightened child' is outside of time, whilst also being perfectly legitimate to say the 'enlightened child' can interact with the human condition that is in time to create amazing results. It is not even a paradox just a thing that the human mind can never understand. Yet the key point within all of this is that as you re-connect more and more to the enlightened child, you realise there is this part of you that can never be broken, never be destroyed and never touched by what happens in the human realm.

This is vitally important, especially when you are healing from trauma. On my own journey healing from severe trauma the factor that made all the difference was my ability to recognise and tap into the 'enlightened child', which made going through even the biggest pain and hurt from the trauma much more manageable. On one hand I could acknowledge how broken I was on a human level. Yet on the other hand I could also see there was part of me that could never be touched by the trauma and was already perfectly fine- I was completely healed and also need of some serious healing at the same time.

The triple healing effect- the more obvious human level, the subtle realm and the 'enlightened child' level

It is really important to get things right when healing on a human level. We need to choose the modality that works best for whatever we are trying to heal.The outer modality we choose (nutrition, traditional medicine, energy healing, psychology, physiotherapy, massage, soul reading, yoga etc) is the 'more obvious human level'. We know what we have signed up for and expect certain things that we associate with it.

What most people don't understand though is that in any given situation when a person is trying to help another person heal there is really a triple healing effect. As well as the more obvious outer human level, there is also the subtle realm and 'enlightened child' level. In the human level there is what we can conceptually understand based on our training or school of thought- for example we may be doing a cognitive psychology session, a nutrition session, a reiki healing session, a counselling session or some medical procedure. It has some sort of science or spiritual understanding behind it. Next there is the subtle realm, which happens in any type of healing or quite frankly any time of relationship (i.e. when you meet with another there is always an energy exchange on some level). This becomes more important during a healing because both parties (especially the illusion of the recipient) are more open. Not as open as during deep sex but open enough to make it more of a factor than during normal interactions. This actually in all cases has more power than the actual modality being performed, although it is hard to grasp this when we are so anchored in the human condition. Even in something like reiki where there is supposed to be more awareness of what is happening in the subtle energy realm, what actually makes much more of the difference is the individual energy fields of the two people involved rather than anything that the reiki energy actually does.

Finally the third factor of the triple healing effect is the 'enlightened child'. This has exponential power far beyond the human realm of what appears to be happening and even far beyond the subtle energy realm too. Unfortunately or maybe fortunately depending on your perspective most people are so disconnected from their own 'enlightened child' that this rarely comes into effect in any great magnitude. You would imagine it depends on the healer's connection to the 'enlightened child' as the primary factor but this would be grossly wrong- it actually depends on the receivers because the healer can only give what the receiver can receive. Before this gets too complicated lets go back to the basics- the key is that there is way more going on in any healing situation than just the formal healing modality, with the two other key factors being the subtle energy realms and the 'enlightened child'.

I don't have much more to say on healing

I honestly thought this chapter would be a lot longer but apparently I am going to have to leave it at that. On my own journey I have performed what would commonly be described as miracles on other people when it comes to healing and I was all pumped up to share them but apparently it is not to be. I am not trying to create mystery here just honesty. As already mentioned I actually found that the more I became embodied in the enlightenment experience the less need there was for 'showy miracles' and the healing could happen in the most down to earth way possible. Often just in conversation and nearly always just in normal life.

Chapter 9-
Enlightenment and Death

Death is by far the biggest fear in the human condition. It is really what we are all running away from through a variety of means- whether that is through achievement, through playing it safe or through avoiding ever facing the reality of death. Just look at funerals for god's sake. I can only comment from the Christian funerals I have attended but what stands out is that no-one is actually prepared to face the reality of death head on- everyone stands there talking about normal life, thinking about death in the most ridiculous means possible (more on this in a minute) and in this passive state where no-one quite knows what to do. We feel a duty to be there but run away from actually facing the reality of what the funeral is all about. Funerals, like most of the human condition, are completely wrapped in our fear of death on every level.

<u>You can only live fully having face death fully</u>
Death is very simple. There are two levels to it- the human level and the 'enlightened child' level. It is beyond obvious that on a human level you are going to die- I mean just look at the evidence from the millions if not billions of people who have died in the last hundreds of years on Earth. You are going to die. There is no escaping that and what gives life its inherent beauty is the fact that you only get one chance in these particular conditions- the particular conditions don't repeat again. You are going to die because the human condition is in time and space, which is always finite. You are going to die.

Yet there is one part of us that is untouchable, which is the 'enlightened child'. I hate how all the spiritual people make such a big song and dance about this in a way that adds stupid mystery that disempowers people. I prefer a more grounded approach. The human part of you is going to die and decay ruthlessly, whilst the 'enlightened child' part of you can never die because it is outside of time and space, which means it is infinite. You are not special though! Everyone has the 'enlightened child' within them, so it is not like 'Jack Prefontaine' survives on any level. He dies completely and will never even be conscious of his death (wow that is painful) but the thing he touched called the 'enlightened child' will stay repeating its creation again and again for the beauty that is life.

This reality of death can be very depressing to begin with. Yet over-time it is the most freeing and live-enhancing thing in the world because it allows you to actually live from the peace, clarity and love of the 'enlightened child'. Love doesn't come from the enlightened child but connecting to it within the realm of the human, allows this very human thing called love to be experienced in its full beauty. Love is much better than peace by the way.

So everyday allow yourself to die- not physically, as you gotta make the most of your time here. But die to the limitations of your human condition. Do something that breaks down your resistance to the re-connection to the 'enlightened child' within you and allow yourself to have a chance to fully die to the wonders of the human condition. The full death of allowing the 'enlightened child' to flow freely is the most beautiful thing in the world and allows you to live to the absolute maximum.

An alternative funeral

Christian funerals have to be the most stupid thing in the whole of existence- even stupider than the twin flame concept perhaps and that is saying something. I mean like seriously who believes that kinda shit? The vicar or whatever the main guy delivering the funeral is called always talks the most total shite I have ever heard in my entire life- he literally tries to makes you believe that the person who is dead is now in this mystical and magical place called heaven, which is only reserved for those who have played by the rules in life. People then imagine something like this…the person in the human form (perhaps a little younger than when they died) floating around in the clouds in heaven having a good time with his family and mates. It is a very comforting thought but also so obviously total shite. Non withstanding the repulsive Christian exclusiveness to this whole heaven thing the person is dead in a coffin or in ashes by this point, so obviously his body is no longer there. He/She/Gender neutral is dead. Perhaps they may be floating around in spirit but that is also so obviously total shite, as it is just a projection of what we are comfortable with in human form into a supposed after life that allows us to escape the fear of death. He/She/Gender neutral is dead.

Then Jesus has to join the party too. Apparently he died to save our sins and give us all this magical chance of joining him in God's kingdom- I mean like seriously Jesus you died over two thousand years ago mate! Can you stop pissing on our parade and being the centre of attention at all these nice people's funerals- feels a little bit egotistical to me. We then also have to sing songs and pretend like we know the words. Most of us haven't been to church for at least a decade but because we are scared of death and want to ensure the person who has died has the best chance in the after-life we turn up full force to the funeral and all guns blazing when it comes to the singing. That is the only part of the funeral where one is allowed to feel an ounce of joy. Outside of that we are told 'we are here to celebrate the life of X', whilst also all having to face the own pain of our own projected fear of death and just generally join in the utter vibration of the misery that is religion.

I should add a disclaimer at this point. The last two paragraphs were written for people generally interested in enlightenment and who want to move beyond the fear of death. There is nothing wrong with feeling pain at a funeral or using the ideas of Christianity to feel better. They have their own place and own merits, adding value to the world. Just don't believe them if you want to re-connect to the 'enlightened child' more and if part of you can see the funny side too then enjoy seeing the absolute absurdity of it.

I am going to have an alternative funeral when I die. It is going to be a big celebration (like a party)- to celebrate any joy people found in my own life but more importantly to celebrate the inherent joy of life itself. No formality, no churches and certainly no religious bollocks- just one big fucking party. Could you imagine how excited people would be? It is easy to get time off work for a funeral but they then become sombre and sad occasions- with my funeral you would be getting time off work to have a shit load of fun and a big party. Way better!

Finale- More enlightened than a jacket potato

If I was to summarise the whole point of this book in a single paragraph this would be my attempt. The current ideas about enlightenment are total bollocks. Harsh but true. A re-connection to the 'enlightened child' within oneself allows you to see past the pretence expounded by so called experts on enlightenment to reveal a very uncomfortable truth. This truth is the total fragility of the human condition. We all walk around life pretending like we know what is happening, whether that be on a worldly level or as we 'advance spiritually' pretending we know what is happening on a spiritual level. Nowhere is this more clear than when one pretends to know about enlightenment. I share my truth. I could be wrong but my own experience tells me that a re-connection to the 'enlightened child' (which is really the highest state of enlightenment possible in the human condition) allows you to be fully human, with a total fragility at your very core. Fragility should not be mistaken for weakness, as it is in fact the ultimate strength. To become fragile is to become fully human, as you fully see your own condition for what it is and also see in others the same fragility being masked by multiple pretences. No-one knows what is going on. Like seriously what is this human life all about? We literally are so plugged into trying to survive and maybe even thrive on a day to day level that we never take time to re-connect to the 'enlightened child' and see the truth that we have absolutely no idea what is going on. A scary realisation. Yet it is only in this fragility and willingness to accept the peace of the 'enlightened child' that one can truly learn to live and most of all learn to accept others with an open heart. You see past all the pretence of the human condition to see the 'enlightened child' in all. On one hand there is this mess of being human that we all have to try to cope with but behind it is something so sacred, so undeniably beautiful and so pure that it can never be touched by any of it. Learn to laugh, learn to accept and maybe even learn to love your humanity but never ever forgot that this life is but a glimpse and a tiny ugly dirty reflection of something so immense, so powerful and so great that no human mind could never imagine it, let alone live it. That is the ultimate mystery. How the total destruction of everything you thought was so true, so solid and so important, allows something so immense to happen that the only way we can describe it is *silence.*

Appendix: 29 unconnected articles from the enlightenment path

Articles 1: Life Lessons

<u>3 key life lessons from talking to the homeless in Exeter as a University student</u>

We so often ignore those who we consider beneath us but I learnt some of my most valuable life lessons by actively engaging with the homeless as a University student.

"Haha look at that pathetic homeless person" my mate sneered, as we walked past a Women with pink hair playing the guitar to earn some money. We all laughed, as we looked forward to a big night out in town. We were freshers after all.

I then made eye contact with the Woman.

It is hard to put into words when moments like these happen but something deep shifted within me. I didn't see a homeless person anymore but instead a vulnerable and worthy human being. I carried on with my mates to the nightclub (peer pressure was too much to do anything drastic in that moment) but made my excuses very early into the night, as I just had to talk to her. Luckily Chloe (like most humans she had a name) was still playing her guitar in the same spot and was a lot more forgiving than I would have been if someone had laughed at me. We got talking.

I learnt all about her life story, including her upbringing, the early career success she had until an abusive husband had destroyed her life and she had been on a downward spiral with drugs and alcohol that meant she ended up living on the streets. Her upbringing and early career success bore much resemblance to my own story- perhaps we are not as different as I thought we were.

From that day onwards I made regular trips out to the homeless in Exeter, giving them hot chocolate and most of all being there for a chat. All those adventures were rich in life lessons- here are the 3 key things I learnt…

1.   Be open to wisdom off everyone

I'm honestly convinced I learnt a lot more talking to the homeless people in Exeter than I did on my degree. These were real life lessons. There is something about being a desperate situation that seems to illuminate profound insights and wisdom in a person, especially when the person manages to look after themselves to a reasonable degree. There were many alcoholics and drug addicts amongst the homeless in Exeter but also those who were doing exceptionally well to stay as healthy as possible in very testing circumstances. It was from these people the wisdom came. One particular highlight was to understand their perspective on how closed and insular people were- the many eyes that looked away when money was asked for, the pretending that they weren't almost human and the sheer arrogance of all those rich students who threw abuse at them as they spent Mummy and Daddy's money on a big night out in Exeter. Luckily I was no longer one of those students.

2.   See beyond the outer appearance

One Saturday morning in my normal routine giving out hot chocolate to the homeless I got talking to Zayn. We were having a lovely chat. He was telling me all about the help a local charity had giving him, his love for Arsenal (his favourite football team) and how he had nearly secured a local job which would mean he was able to see his six-year-old son again. I felt a lot of love for him to be honest. This was quite a big breakthrough moment for me, as I had seen him a couple of times before, but had been scared to approach him. You see Zayn was well above six foot, with huge bulging muscles, tattoos all over his body (including his face) and with a local reputation from some of the other homeless people of being a thug not be messed with. Perhaps he did have a different side to him but that morning all I could see was a kind man trying to do the best with his life.

3.   Your time and attention is the greatest gift you can give someone

There were different organisations who would give food to the homeless in Exeter. They generally did it differently to how I did it though. More almost like feeding an animal at the zoo and being scared to have a proper chat, which is what the homeless people all repeatedly told me. I realised the hot chocolate was just a symbol. Merely a convenient starting point to say "hey mate I care" and am prepared to give you some of my time to hear your story and have a chat. Often in life we are so focused on achievements for us and others that we forget that what people most really want is to know that we care and are worthy of their time.

5 things I learnt from running a 31-mile ultramarathon aged 20

I needed a crazy freshers week challenge after the journey I had been on. From hitting rock bottom aged 18, where I was off school for 4 months with chronic fatigue, I had managed to recover to the point that I could exercise fully again. Having formerly been a top 50 UK distance runner for my age group, I knew it had to involve running further than I had ever done before. Maybe a half-marathon? Maybe a 20 miler? Or maybe even a full marathon?

I went bigger, completing a 31-mile ultramarathon (with over 3,000 ft of ascent) during freshers week at the University of Exeter, with constant laps around the main hilly campus. It took around 6 hours but the memories and lesson learnt were enough to last a lifetime. Here are the 5 key things I learnt...

1.   Your potential is much more than you believe

The real barrier is the mind and self-imposed limiting beliefs. Between miles 15-26 it was extremely tough going and there were many moments where it felt like finishing would be absolutely impossible. My mind (and parts of my body!) told me to stop. When I broke through the marathon barrier, however, it was like something switched in my mind and the body responded accordingly. I was on the way home now. It was amazing to see how much more energy I suddenly had through this shift in mindset and it was like I was accessing energy that previously had been impossible to touch. Cool doesn't even begin to describe 10% of it! I honestly believe I could have gone much further than 31 mils with the energy I had, which was crazy considering how tired I felt during parts of it before.

2.   Support is critical

There was no way I would have got through those tough miles 15-26 if I hadn't been supported by friends running with me for the odd lap or two. The same applies to life. No-one ever achieved extraordinary things without significant support and a great team around them.

3.   The mind is incredibly focused after intense exercise

I had a lecture in the afternoon and was feeling so good from my morning run that I went along. I have never got a bigger buzz or been more focused on the intricates of human physiology than I was that day. For stunning academic results or feats of mind it is absolutely essential we look after our body to the maximum. Admittedly I did completely crash with about 10 minutes to go in the lecture but I will excuse myself since I had ran an ultramarathon!

4.   We are human

Holy shamoly my body the hurt the next day and still quite intensely for like two weeks after my efforts. My calf muscle in particular would keep cramping up on a daily basis and I was never convinced my left knee was the same after. I hadn't done any proper training in the few months leading up to it...I went more for mindset and being well-rested, as well as my natural athletic ability, to ensure I got through. Often in life when we try to achieve extraordinary things we can forget the very ordinary and human aspect of ourselves. I learnt from this to be more gentle towards those aspects and always take them into account.

5.   Sometimes crazy things heal the most

There is a temptation on a healing path to make it all too safe. This ultramarathon was the final release of all the worry and stress that the chronic fatigue had brought into my life. It showed me I could trust my energy levels even in extreme situations and also fully recover from intense physical endeavours. Most people will seek the next big running challenge after something like this but I was very content and happy to barely run again after it.

<u>I changed my name to Jay-Jay Masters for a month- here are 10 key life lessons it taught me</u>
On my recovery from trauma a spiritual master, who had helped me a lot, suggested I change my name to Jay-Jay Masters.

Here are the hilarious results of a month-long name change experiment.

Experiments are fun. Experiments when you change your name for a month are even more interesting.

Looking back now I can laugh but at the time I was so determined to heal from trauma that I was prepared to try anything. Even the wacky, unusual and downright bizarre. And I trusted man. The spiritual master who suggested the name change had helped me on a very deep level - he was a best-selling Hay House author and an expert in his field so he had pedigree too.

Jay-Jay Masters was ready to be unleashed on the world.

1.   It isn't ideal to change your name as a sports coach half-way through the season

I was coaching the Blues teams at Oxford University at this point, so it was very prestigious and stiff upper lip. They had just about coped with Jack Prefontaine but Jay-Jay Masters was going to be a whole new level. How could I share about the name change? I thought it would be better to introduce it to the Ladies team first, as they were likely to be far less savage about it then the men. I went for the casual technique. "Just a little bit of admin," I shared with the girls in the pre-game team talk, as I normally did. Admin normally meant timings, updates about training, selection. Name changes didn't quite traditionally fit into that scope. "I have made the decision to change my name to Jay-Jay," I shared in the most casual tone possible, "so I think it is better if you call me that". They burst out laughing. This was far more exciting than the normal pre-game admin! A thousand questions followed but we had a game to prepare for, so I pushed them away. Inevitably we made our worst start to a game of the entire season, as their minds were still much more focused on the sudden name change of their coach than winning a hockey match.

2.   Jay-Jay Masters spreads quickly

Maybe it is something unique to the Jay-Jay's of this world but news of my name change spread rapidly around the hockey club. Maybe this was a blessing because I didn't have to tell the Men, as they already knew.

3.   It can be fun having two identities

For the rest of the season it became a running joke to compare the contrasting characters of Jay-Jay and Jack. Anything beautiful we could associate to Jay-Jay, while all the less desirable characteristics could be attributed to Jack. Him and his old ways hey! This gave me a lot of freedom and was very entertaining.

4. Changing your name insults your parents

I should have seen this one coming from a mile off. I mean Jack was their choice after all! It was personal to them! My Mum was particularly distraught, whilst my Dad tried to find the positives that this could help him "find himself". It was unclear whether I was trying to find Jack or Jay-Jay at this point but I appreciated his positivity nevertheless.

5. You find your real friends

Some friends will back you through anything, even obscure off the cuff name changes! Some will find it too weird and won't want to be friends with you anymore. Having said that maybe they just didn't like Jay-Jay but would re-consider about Jack?

6. Formal identities can be real party poopers

The lady behind the desk at the train station was confused. "Your saying your name is Jay-Jay but you want to renew your railcard for Jack Prefontaine?" she questioned, looking at me as though I should be placed in a mental asylum. Maybe for real success one needs to formally change one's name too.

7. Social Media becomes a hassle

How do you explain a facebook update where your name suddenly changes from "Jack Prefontaine" to "Jay-Jay Masters"? It either looks like a quarter-life crisis or a fraud scheme- neither giving good looks.

8. It doesn't enhance your business reputation

Another issue was I had spiritual and healing clients at this point. It is hard to build trust when the client can't even be sure you will have the same name week on week. Jay-Jay Masters certainly wasn't a money magnet is all I can say.

9. Spiritual Masters really don't have it all sorted

It is often best in life just to use common sense. I mean perhaps there were some hidden profound spiritual lessons to be discovered from changing my name (oh the illusion of identity) but it was rather a car-crash month to be honest. Always be sceptical and see that even the most "advanced spiritually" will have personal biases and human flaws.

10. If you are going to change your name go for something much better than Jay-Jay Masters

Annoyingly the Spiritual Master suggested this name but looking back I could have had so much fun. The whole world of names was my oyster. And I went for "Jay-Jay Masters"! A middle-aged bird from the local golf course? I should have gone for something like "Dixie Normus" or "Ben Dover" or "Legend Prefontaine" (honouring the legend that was Steve Prefontaine). I eventually realised plain old Jack Prefontaine suited me just fine.

Radical Acceptance= 20 press ups

Press ups have never been my strong point.

Like everyone some things come naturally to me and other things don't. I became a top 50 UK cross-country runner for my age group as a teenager without doing anything extraordinary training-wise, whilst in contrast I would have probably made the bottom 50 of press-ups for my age group. Ok maybe that's a slight exaggeration. I could still beat the fat Freds, porky Peters and lazy Lukes but relative to my overall athletic prowess my press-ups were really poor.

My PB as a teenager was 12. And it was a dodgy 12 too.

So I set myself a challenge three months ago to smash through new barriers with my press-ups... new frontiers that very few human beings have explored. Ok well maybe 50 press-ups wasn't that unique in the human world but it was a big deal to me! I was a man now. No more weedy teenage arms that were under-developed compared to his peers (but perfect for long distance running), I was now a fully grown 26 year-old male with slightly below average arm size but still bigger than the weedy teenager!

It was time for the "press-up experiment".

As a side-point this was way more interesting than any spiritual experiment I had ever done and it generally offered deeper life lessons than the average spiritual retreat I had been on. When in Rome as they say.

I made an extremely strong start. I didn't break my personal Jack record the first week but week two was a big break-through week…it was generally a surprise to me that Sky Sports News weren't in touch for an exclusive, such was the scale of my achievement. I didn't just break my personal Jack record, I smashed little weak teenage Jack out of the park!

20 PRESS UPS (NEW JACK RECORD!!!!)

I wanted to cry, I wanted to thank everyone who had supported me on this journey with so much sacrifice along the way and I wanted to remember all the pain of only been able to do 12 press-ups as a teenager that had made this journey all worth it. But I was also greedy. My aim wasn't simply to hover at the 20 press-up mark no matter how mind-shattering that achievement was, I wanted to go further than Everest and reach the peak of the 50 press-up mark. Could this kid even be considered human if he reached the magic 50?

My body didn't obey.

Perhaps one of my old spiritual masters had put the "20 press-ups curse" on me but that is only mere speculation. All I can do is report back. I tried everything- more training, more rest, different types of press-ups, different types of other upper body exercise, praying to God, asking my Mum for help but nothing worked. I plateaued for a solid 6 weeks at the now unmagical 20 mark.

I was angry, frustrated and annoyed at my stupid weak little arms. Then I remembered that I was supposed to be "spiritually awake" (vom what a horrible term) and from then on there was only one noble way out of this life dilemma.

Should I continue to suffer for another month in the hope of hitting the elusive 21 (50 was well out of my mind by this point) or could I just accept my body how it was and give up from a place of radical acceptance?

I chose the latter option. Some spiritual people say radical acceptance is accepting one's trauma but I can tell them for free there is nothing more traumatic than not being able to make any progress in your press-up practice for 6 weeks. It hurts not just your arms but your pride too.

But such is the way in the spiritual life- no grand promises are made in the realm of how many press ups one can do but one can be sure that with decent amounts of spiritual practice you can always accept your limitations. Perhaps there is a life lesson in that somewhere.

Articles 2: Meditation
Meditating Naked

We should all be meditating naked.

No not literally you cheeky little rascal! I mean in how we approach our meditation inwardly, which then outwardly approaches as an exciting naked approach to life.

Like how they approach life most spiritual people meditate in a rigid, limiting and clothed way. This is not good for enlightenment. This is not good for finding joy in life. This is not good for finding peace in meditation.

So what does a naked inwardly meditation feel like? There are three key aspects...

Allow everything to be there

We are not trying to find peace in meditation, we are trying to find life. It is vital to soften and relax to allow everything to be invited to the meditation party- your deepest joy, your deepest sorrow, your love, your anger and much more. All is welcome. What often happens is people close their emotional field during meditation in the hope of finding some sort of pseudo peace, which completely limits them in every way in the long-run. We need our emotional field open. Sometimes nothing may happen and it may be the most boring meditation in the history of humanity, whilst at other times it may be more emotional and passionate than the best sex of your life. You don't know. Your job is to simply be open to the possibilities.

Be consistent but not rigid

For meditation to have some sort of effect we do need to show up to the meditation jungle each day. There has to be a consistency. Yet this consistency should never turn into a rigidity, which results in a staleness and a meditation as about as dynamic as a tin of baked beans. There is a discipline but only in the framework of a real indiscipline. You need to be grounded and anchored in an intent that you love your meditation enough for its fire to change you from within but not so grounded and anchored that the fire can only spread to small parts of your story. We want all the stories to be burnt alive!

Be soft and tender

Meditation can hurt man. Often spiritual people hold a phenomenal amount of inner tension from trying to make their meditation a certain way or live up to a certain standard, which stops all the beauty of softness and tenderness entering the meditation equation. Be softer than the sweetest rose. Be more tender than the most loving relationship. Be more vulnerable than a new born baby into the world.

The one meditation technique that will change your life

Meditation is delicious.

This is especially the case when a meditation technique has the potential to completely change your life, as the one I am about to share does. This is powerful stuff. It is not the normal meditations found in the standard meditation apps or in those nice peaceful meditation classes that make everyone feel happy and smiley. This is deep shit bro.

Right let the grand unveil take place...

In normal life centre yourself by breathing into the lower abdomen area. Then imagine that instead of the world coming at you and being all real, it is in fact coming from your own mind (like a dream) and isn't real at all. It is just your dream and what you are perceiving is completely a projection of your own mind.

This breaks the ego thought system at the deepest level. It isn't real, it isn't real, it isn't real. It puts you in a place of not knowing and also not taking everything so darn seriously. There is nothing better for authentic confidence, inner peace and getting into a state of flow. It relaxes you back to the centre of real life and allows you to let things unfold a lot more naturally from a centred place within.

Right grand unveil (v2) to super-power this meditation even more...

Using the same meditation technique replace what you think you are seeing with the body's eyes to only see "the light" within each individual. By the "the light" I mean visually a white light at the centre of their heart, which is full of peace, purity and real purpose. You can also try it on objects, though it works better on human beings because they trigger a lot of stories in us. Especially those who you know well.

This takes you from touching some of the things such as authentic confidence, inner peace and flow into being able to stay consistent in them for much longer periods of time. No gawping though! You are like a meditation super-agent sent into the combat of real life to discover all these amazing thing within yourself.

This meditation technique works so well because it touches a very deep truth that what you see is entirely a projection of your own mind. The first step helps take you out of the firm grip of your own projections and the second step helps replace your natural projection with something that is going to serve you much better if peace, happiness and flow is something you legit want.

Enjoy fellow meditator and fucking smash life!

3 Shocking Reflections About The Spiritual World From A High Performance Sports Coach

After the sudden breakdown of my life in my early-20s I invested a few intense years in the spiritual world. Here are three shocking reflection from what I found...

The spiritual world is as corrupt as the corporate world, if not more so

I had a childlike purity of innocence about the spiritual world. Here were people full of peace, who had my best interests at heart and who I could trust. I was wrong. It turns out the spiritual world is just as corrupt as the corporate world, being full of good people but also people who will take advantage of you, disempower you for personal gain and lie to protect their self-interest. I actually feel it is much uglier than the corporate world. At least there is a fundamental honesty about the corporate world in that it is about profit and making money, in comparison to the spiritual world which loves to hide behind grand and pure sounding statements that hide the truth about the incredible human aspects of it. And that is really the crux of this whole point. The spiritual world and corporate world are the same because they are full of exactly the same mixture of imperfect human beings. The only difference is the spiritual world just escapes from this reality more.

Most of spirituality is just a cyclical process that continues to play out your pain in a spiritual context

Fundamentally the whole point of spirituality is acceptance of your human story and re-discovering the innocence behind all of this. It is so incredibly simple it often baffles me what all the fuss is about. The problem is no-one in the spiritual world really wants to accept this point (unless they actually want to touch their deepest pain and full innocence) because to do so would destroy the whole purpose and meaning behind their spirituality, as well as put them in much closer contact with their pain. So much of spirituality is just a mask and better sounding way to play out/avoid pain in a different setting. Like the person in an abusive and disempowering relationship who then plays it out with their relationship to their spiritual teacher, or the person who escapes their pain through sex and alcohol but then just escapes

123

it through being a "starseed" or "ascending to 5-D" or the person who feels lonely so they find solace in a spiritual community who "really understands them" (not like all those idiots in the normal world). It is just rejection after rejection, running away after running away, avoidance after avoidance of PAIN&PEACE.

Most spiritual people (including teachers/masters) are in trauma and use spirituality to escape their pain and the world

I know this point at a very deep level because this is exactly what I did, as well as seeing it even in other people in the spiritual world. Spirituality is such a convenient escape from human pain and trauma. It makes it all sound more noble, more pure and more loving when the reality is, we are nearly all just hurt human beings struggling to find our way in lives. Sorry to burst the bubble but this is so important. It allows you to see through all the glorification of a multitude of concepts and ideas in the spiritual world and gives you a much better chance of not only fully looking at your pain/trauma but also through this process discovering the innocence and peace that was always there. It was just all the spirituality was blocking it.

10 naughty things about the spiritual world I would tell a 10-year-old Jack

Never trust a psychic called Eileen- aged 20 she told me I would be a millionaire by aged 23. I am still waiting aged 27 for my first 100k let alone 1 million.

The spiritual gurus/masters love fucking their students but never talk about sex- age 10 is about the time you first have sex education, so I think this is just about legit. There are many spiritual gurus/masters who love to take advantage of their positions of power by engaging in sexual relationships with pupils but then confusingly never talk about sex, like it is not part of the spiritual path or the human condition. Perhaps they are hiding an inconvenient truth.

Qualifying as a yoga teacher makes you much more attractive to the opposite sex- you appear more spiritual, flexible in all the right areas and maybe even a little enlightened too.

Spirituality is a business- don't be fooled little Jack that spirituality is this pure thing above the human need for money, power and control. It is actually often much worse than the corporate world.

Leicester City will win the title in the 2015/16 season against 10,000-1 odds- if you put £100 on Leicester City winning the title in the 2015/16 season you will become a millionaire and prove Eileen right.

Some spiritual people use their magical powers for bad- they use things like energy healing, yoga, tantra and their "ability to change the weather" to get control over other people, disempowering them in the name of spiritual enlightenment.

Don't follow older adults, especially spiritual masters/gurus- it can sometimes be helpful little Jack to get support on your spiritual path but never become a follower. Always stand in your own authority and encourage others to do the same.

There is nothing sacred about Jesus or your Christian religion- just think about it logically little Jack. Why would you follow a man who was so hated that he got crucified when he was barely out of his 30s? You should have higher aspirations for your life.

Find a beautiful Women not your twin flame- twin flames are dangerous creatures. Just try to find a beautiful Women who is kind, fun and down to earth.

Never believe in fairies, angels, goddesses (or Santa Claus) - spiritual people like to make things up outside of the human condition to make them feel safe and good about themselves. Don't believe them little Jack. Just enjoy your life and try to be a kind person who helps others in the world.

<u>10 spiritual concepts that I don't believe</u>

Divine Love- I really feel love is a very human thing. So tender, so gentle and so humanly heart-opening that I don't see why divinity has to come and spoil the imperfectly perfect human party.

Astrology- oh where to begin? Don't get me wrong there is something in it if understood deeply but seriously how superficial is most of the astrology we see. Like a sun sign could give so much information on you. Individuals are infinitely more complex and even then it is just a human story.

Law of attraction- lots of people of my generation love this one. "I attracted this", "I manifested this", "I changed this belief to get X into my life". This is empowering up to a point as it helps you start to grasp that the real power is within you but as you progress on your spiritual journey it becomes rather disempowering and a lot of ego-focused effort. And I feel it all goes back to one thing for people who tend to be obsessed with this sort of stuff. They can't accept failure or the imperfect parts of themselves, so they are constantly striving to paper over the cracks. I am a big fan of trying to be successful but perhaps with a little more humility and realising some things aren't actually in your control.

Spiritual people- there are only human beings.

The 7 Chakras- people don't even seem to question the existence of the 7 chakras now it is so deeply woven into the spiritual community. But honestly I have never located one. I did loads of energy training with spiritual teachers/masters, am a qualified yoga teacher and have done hundreds of healing sessions with clients but chakras have always seemed to escape my awareness. Maybe I am just not spiritual enough to see one yet.

Spiritual Gurus/Masters- oh these are always the funniest type of people. So perfect, so pure and just there to help humans like me and you escape from our human limitations. What utter bollocks! There is no doubt one can discover some deep spiritual things and want to share them with others (I did) but to have to use it in such an authoritarian way is so old school. They are all human! I am looking forward to the concept of masters/gurus being banished in the 21st century.

Sacredness- those scared scriptures, those sacred spiritual objects, those sacred spiritual books, those sacred spiritual places. The only thing that is sacred is the silence not of this world.

Oneness- along with chakras and the law of attraction this has to be the biggest load of spiritual hogwash in the spiritual community currently. "We are all one". "There is only oneness". "Oneness is true reality". I mean like come on? At a deeper level there is something to re-discover within oneself but I don't see oneness as a suitable description on any level, especially when

126

you consider how most spiritual people really use it. Oneness makes it all appear so above the reality of human existence on one hand but also like the very fabric of spirituality is woven into this world in some coherent way. It would be better instead to embrace the duality of what it means to be human and live life to the full, whilst also re-connecting to the nothingness at the same time that breaks all meaning.

Spiritual Evolution- quite a thing these days, especially in the alternative healing communities. Again it all goes back to why can't you just be human? Why can't you accept how you are? Why do you have to evolve beyond what you are? Is there something wrong with you? Is there something superior about you compared to unevolved humans? Evolution in life is valid and important but spiritually the best evolution is the dynamic collapse of the whole evolutionary process.

Divine Feminine- I mean without being cheeky females are just absolutely divine exactly how they are. Like why put spirituality in the way of the inherent beauty of Women? Female empowerment is a topic close to my heart and something I feel is really important to keep developing in the world but I don't think the Divine Feminine spiritual concept needs to interfere with all of this.

Approaching Spirtuality From A Positive Place

Have you ever heard of the person who is rich, has great family/friends, loves their career, loves their intimate relationships and has great flow to their life who then suddenly out of nowhere gets interested in spirituality?

I certainly haven't.

Most people come to spirituality because something has gone wrong in their life- whether that is a broken relationship, no meaning in their career or deep-seated trauma that makes them not want to be in this world.

This creates an issue.

I would suggest that nearly all of the spiritual world and by implication the people in it are approaching their spirituality from quite a negative place. I certainly did for a long time. By this I mean spirituality becomes a mechanism through one which can escape all the pain and hurt in one's life through concepts such as "divine love", "oneness" and "5-D ascension".

127

Spirituality becomes an escape.

Now spiritual escapism is "a thing" in the spiritual world but I honestly don't feel anyone sees to any degree how deep this issue really is.

Real spirituality destroys your negative spirituality.

This is why I always emphasise positive things in the world- vibrant health, loving relationships and career success. For some people this won't seem like "real spirituality" where it is all about going beyond the world and discovering "our true nature" but really when deeply understood I feel it is an essential part of any deep sharing. It anchors you into life. And stops the tendency in nearly all spiritual seekers to run and escape as much as possible from the real pain and human hurt they are feeling inside.

The human hurt and pain is really the doorway to the spirituality we all seek.

You would think it is the opposite. I admire and respect spiritual teachers/masters who want to focus on "the infinite", "oneness", "our true nature" but this can only be truly achieved with a radical and deep understanding of what it means to be fully human. And fully alive.

And they can't do this because they haven't really discovered it within themselves and are instead projecting their own negative spirituality onto those who seek their help.

I say love life.

Love money, love sex, love success, love your pain, love your limitations, love your achievements, love your setbacks, love your sorrow, love the love of your life, love your friends, love your family.

Then spirituality takes on a whole new meaning and becomes a deeper celebration in tune with both a fantastic human life and the silence that permeates it all.

Build a beautiful community outside of your spirituality

We all need connection as human beings. Ok bar maybe the enlightened yogis from way back who just hung out in caves on their own for decades on end but seriously who wants to live a life like them? So boring and like 10th century shit.

As spiritual people our search for connection often becomes even more intense, with many people determined to find "like-

128

minded" people and become part of some sort of "spiritual community". You know all that "find your tribe" kinda vibe.

I believe in the power of community- we all need it as human beings but even more so as we encounter some of our more vulnerable human pain on the spiritual path. We don't need spiritual community though. Especially those spiritual communities that try to take you away from "3-D Reality", away from "your negative family and friends" and from "people who just don't get you".

Obviously at some points it is important to move on from certain negative people in our life and I am not for one moment suggesting inertia but I do feel there needs to be some perspective. Spiritual communities are dangerous in my opinion. They take you away from your own beautiful community that best serves you as the unique human being you are and also massively reduce your spiritual development. True spirituality can only really be found in collaboration (which very few if any spiritual communities really are) and in embracing all aspects of life (which all spiritual communities reject overtly or subtly).

So how does one build a beautiful community outside of their spirituality? I feel there are three key points...

Surround yourself with friends who fill different needs for you

You must be one heck of a boring person if you only have "spiritual friends". It would limit the perspective you have on life and stop you from fully embracing all parts of yourself that need to be nourished and honoured. I have friends who I have deep spiritual conversations with, friends I talk to about sport, friends I talk about sex/relationships, friends who I talk to a lot about career/business things and friends who I joke around a lot with about really stupid things. It is highly doubtful one friend could give you everything you need, so it is best to embrace all types of friends who make you feel good and add value to your life.

Love your family

My family aren't spiritual at all- not in anyway really. They are not interested in it, don't want to talk about it and find it all rather weird if I am honest. I respect that. They (Mum/Dad/Sister) add a lot of value and love into my life in other ways, so it is best to embrace those parts than worrying about the parts they can't provide. Often it is tempting on a spiritual path to reject our family or even blame them for some of the things we don't like about ourselves but that is just really spiritually immature. In fact your family, especially parents, are often your greatest teachers. Once you can come from a place of true inner peace and unconditional love towards them, then you really are getting somewhere on the enlightenment path.

See the spirituality in everything

Like seriously what is the difference between a spiritual person and a non-spiritual person. With true inner vison surely everyone just looks the same anyway? Now that would be radical. Radical. You see as we mature on our spiritual journey an incredible, slightly naughty and spicy, fact starts to dawn on us... we should just choose our community based in what meets our human needs, rather than any illusion about a community to enhance my spirituality.

And this is the great illusion isn't it? Those who search for their tribe in a spiritual community are really just trying to have their human needs met.

This is why I again emphasise it is such a bad way to progress spiritually to join a spiritual community because all the human needs get mixed up rather complicatedly with the need for some sort of spiritual enlightenment. This is why so many fucked up things always happen in spiritual communities.

So be bold, be worldly and be modern - build a beautiful and diverse human community around you, so you can then fully explore your spirituality in normal life.

<u>Confessions of an average yogi</u>

Yoga tradition has some very rigid habits. Here I confess too some naughty "bad yogic habits", which I feel have actually enhanced my well-being.

My yoga teacher training was intense. Four weeks of getting up at 5am in the morning for practice, a strictly vegetarian diet and periods of silence to help us go deeper within. It that wasn't enough we were only allowed mobile phones for one hour per day, weren't allowed to talk during meals (so we could be present with our food) and had ten hours a day of education, including posture practice, meditation and theory work. This was all combined of course with the obvious chastity. I managed to

130

qualify as a teacher. However, I couldn't help but wonder if all these rigid yogic habits were really good for my health and well-being, as they put a lot of subtle pressure on you and tended to prey on perfectionist habits.

It didn't take long for me to "break" in the real world. Here I would like to share some confessions, as an average yogi, on some naughty habits that I actually feel have enhanced by health and well-being despite not being in the traditional yogic textbook.

Sleeping as much as I need- I could never quite work out why the yogis from ancient times were so obsessed with getting up for practice at 3am. Apparently it was the perfect time to "connect with higher frequencies", whatever that means. We even tried it a couple of times on our yoga training, not that it made much difference since we were always getting up at 5am anyway. It was clear to me that during the training our physical performance in practice started to decline a few days in. It was obvious from my Sports Science degree why this was. We simply were not recovering enough from our large amounts of physical work each day, with the lack of sleep being the number one cause of this. Perhaps I wasn't spiritual enough to wake up early each morning but I certainly found my health, well-being and overall performance in all areas started to dramatically improve once I was sleeping as much as I needed again.

Skipping more than the odd day of practice- I mean like seriously, who has time to do two hours of proper yoga practice each day? I certainly didn't. Similar to the point above it also tended to lead to over-training and was quite frankly rather boring compared to a variety of exercise to include not only yoga but sometimes running, bodyweight exercises or gym in the morning too.

Eating animal products- having ate raw vegan, vegan, vegetarian and normal standard Western I have deep experience of using a wide variety of diets to get optimal health. The yogic diet can make you feel guilty for not eating a certain "perfect way". I find the best diet for me was a healthy standard Western diet, enjoying foods I loved eating to the max and not stressing about the details of it.

Being angry sometimes- there is nothing like a healthy dose of anger to release some old wounds and let out normal human frustrations. Yoga communities are often full of superficiality. A superficial peace, a superficial kindness and a superficial love that is not only very annoying but also really not very good for your health and well-being.

Enjoying Sex- yoga sometimes makes you feel guilty about having sex, like chastity is the only way to purification and perfection. I think it would be fair to say though that the vast majority of people find well-being (and pleasure) benefits from having sex, so it seems silly to cut it all out in the name of some "ideal".

Saying "thanks guys" not "namaste"- I always made a point at the end of my yoga classes just to say "thank guys". There is always that awkward moment in a class where everyone gets up from lying down, sits in a meditation posture and faces you in prayer hands position at the front of the class. Those in the know are just waiting to sequel "namaste" to demonstrate how advanced their yoga is and how pure their practice has made them. So it was always fun to just say "thanks guys" in the most brummy accent I could muster, which often brought things straight back down to Earth.

Being on technology for more than one hour a day- I mean very few people can live on one hour or less of technology a day in the modern world. And you know what? I kind of enjoyed falling in love with my trusty mobile phone, my reliable laptop and the football on the television again. It made me feel human and properly free again.

<u>What helping Females heal and develop spiritually has taught me about female empowerment</u>

Often as a male it is easy to be confused or maybe even cynical about Female Empowerment. My experiences in healing and spiritual coaching have taught me to look with fresh eyes.

Sometimes in life it is important to go outside your comfort zone. That is exactly what I told myself as I prepared for my first ever female client, in my newly found gift of helping others with their spirituality and healing.

It just so happened that there was more than a 50 year age gap between us- me the former young High Performance Sports

Coach aged 24 years old and Angela, my first female client, aged 76 years old and long retired. Age is just a number.

I will leave the exact details of the work I did with Angela private for obvious reasons but what I would like to share is my experiences with female empowerment from all the clients I have worked with in the last couple of years. Out of the roughly 200 clients I have worked with, the vast majority have been female and also over 35. It has taught me a huge amount about female empowerment, which I summarise in three key lessons below...

1. Both genders have a role to play in female empowerment

I have a confession to make. I am not a fan of this whole female empowerment vibe where it becomes a females only thing (with often subtle undertones of man-hating). We need to be working together. Ultimately there is much to be gained for both genders in supporting female empowerment, as obviously it helps Women step into their full potential but less obviously also helps men learn the most they can from Women. There is real power in a Women being vulnerable towards a man and vice-versa. I often felt one of the key reasons for my success with my female clients wasn't so much the specifics of what I did but the fact that I was a young male who could hold a good space and help them re-evaluate some of the assumptions they held about men which concealed deeply held pain.

2. A lot of the blocks seem to be around leadership

I'm not exactly sure why this is to be honest but if I was to hazard a guess I would say it goes a lot to childhood conditioning and lazy stereotypes about what leadership actually entails. Often Women completely under-value their leadership potential, which stops them becoming fully empowered. Real leadership isn't shouting and being dictatorial towards people but in listening and getting people on board behind a common well thought out vision. Women often have much better natural attributes to excel in this compared to Men in my experience but will rarely feel that way or see their full potential.

Female Empowerment really should be a topic we focus on

I feel it is sometimes easy as a man to get cynical or even a little frustrated with this whole female empowerment movement.

Especially when it feels like an attack against men, as already discussed. Like in any debate or movement there are always going to be different factions but all the client work has certainly taught me this is not a topic to be taken lightly and one where is still much more work to be done.

Articles 4: Steve Prefontaine

3 things we can all learn from Steve Prefontaine

Steve Prefontaine was unique. He never won an Olympic medal and never set a World Record but he inspired thousands if not millions with his unique spirit. Although his athletic accomplishments were impressive, especially considering he never lived to run in his prime, what made Steve Prefontaine so great was something else entirely. It was his spirit.

Here are 3 things we can all learn from Steve Prefontaine...

Run out hard in front

So many of us live a life dominated by following others- with their rules and at their pace. In his running career Steve Prefontaine defined conventional wisdom by always running as fast as he could and running from the front, instead of staying in the pack and kicking towards the end of the race. We need to do the same in our own lives.

Live courageously, live our own uniqueness and live by running hard from the front. Others may catch us eventually but it is far more fun to live this way.

Live your passion not what makes you money

Steve Prefontaine lived on food stamps most of his life. That's right! One of the best and most famous athletes in America in the 1970s was living on the poverty line because of amateur status for athletes at the time. He could have made way more money elsewhere from giving up his dream of an Olympic Gold Medal but instead he decided to do what he loved for a living.

I am always a big advocate of financial abundance and enjoying the material side of life no matter how spiritual or enlightened you are/want to be. Yet sometimes the Universe doesn't provide. Even if you are the master of the law of attraction and the secret I repeat the Universe doesn't always provide. It's called a more advanced spiritual lesson. Where you just let go of your need for money and material comfort by going into the unknown to follow your passion. Just like Steve did.

Speak out

Steve Prefontaine spoke out. He spoke out against the amateur governing bodies of America and how they were making tons of money off him, whilst him and his fellow athletes lived in poverty. He wasn't afraid of authority. What was right was more important to him.

Speaking out takes bravery and courage. Yet as one goes deeper on the spiritual path it becomes easier because you realise that being liked by everyone matters little and that the deeper protection comes from the peace you connect too inside. It is not speaking out to be rebellious (that's just immature) but instead speaking out to inspire others to follow their heart and raise issues that are close to your own heart. We need more outspoken characters like Prefontaine.

3 Steve Prefontaine Quotes To Set Your Spiritual Pants On Fire

It was love at first sight. Aged 14 I watched the movie on Steve Prefontaine's life and fell in love with the man, as well as the legend. "Go Pre, go Pre, go Pre".

Here are 3 amazing Steve Prefontaine quotes to set your spiritual pants on fire, with a little explanation from me on each one...

"To give anything less than your best is to sacrifice the gift"

OMG! My favourite quote of all time. To me the gift is "the gift of peace", that state of innocence, complete peace and child-like wonder we are all trying to re-discover on the spiritual path. You should always give your best to obtain this universal gift.

"I have a positive mental attitude, and I think I'm divine, but I also think it takes a heck of a lot of blood, sweat and tears"

A positive mindset and feeling divine can only take you so far on the spiritual path. Ultimately we are looking for a feminine gentleness and peace within combined with the masculine warrior nature of blood, sweat and tears.

"I do it because I can, I can because I want to, I want to because you said I couldn't"

Sometimes the doubts of others fuels our own inner fire. Many people will doubt you on the spiritual path and many will try to make you feel small by disempowering you with their "spiritual greatness" but I believe you can shine radiantly as the unique individual you are.

How the spirit of Steve Prefontaine can inspire us all

Steve Prefontaine was running on spirit more than anything else. He lit up the often boring and mechanical world of distance running with his charisma, passion for life and rebellious nature. Here are some ways the spirit of Steve Prefontaine can inspire us all…

Always invest in a last chance

Distance running was the last chance Steve Prefontaine had to make his name at something. He was too small for American Football and not agile enough for basketball, so he came to long distance running aged thirteen knowing that this was his last chance to make it at sport. And perhaps even in life, considering the normal prospects of someone who came from his region in Oregon. He was highly doubted. Many people thought he was too small, not tough enough and wouldn't have the speed but he proved everyone wrong.

How many times is it true that we fail and fail but then suddenly we get our break just when we are about to give up? This is often documented as happening in many big breakthroughs or the lives of successful people but perhaps what is under-documented is the multitude of unheard people who give up just before they are really going to make it at something. The key is showing up with a healthy dose of realism. If you show up with your maximum intent to everything and reflect with realism about your aptitude for a certain activity, you will sure bet that over time you will find your niche. Yet often only after a lot of failure. Sometimes the universe wants to push us to breaking point to see how far we are really prepared to go, before presenting a path that starts to make sense when we see all the prior learning was needed for us to thrive in it. So if you are on the cusp of giving up, always give things one last chance until you find your niche just like Steve did.

Be honestly focused if you want success

Steve Prefontaine was notoriously viewed as being quite an abrasive and cocky character. Was this really true though? Those who knew him more seemed to consider that actually all the behaviour that would be considered abrasive and cocky to some was just a fundamental honesty that his primary focus was being the best runner he could be and nothing else. You really can't please everybody. Steve Prefontaine is a great example of someone not only talked the talk but also walked the walk because behind the outer bravado was someone deeply in love and committed to their craft. His two workouts a day with huge weekly mileage are legendary. This is not only a testament to his relentless pursuit for greatness but also the incredible 'off the track' balance he must have had to maintain this mileage without any serious injuries throughout the entirety of our career.

If we want to be successful we must be honestly focused on what we really want and then take consistent action that is completely aligned with this vision. This will upset people. The vast majority of people have zero interest in ever living a life of greatness and have certain unwritten expectations over how one must act towards them, even if it is not aligned with you following your own greatness. Don't look for conflict but be prepared to stay firm when it inevitably comes. If you really want to be bold and go for things don't be afraid of shouting your own trumpet and sharing your greatness with the world (if you have put the serious work in behind it). Often people with true greatness are quite shy and hesitant to share (even Steve Prefontaine wasn't confident as a teenager), whilst those with limited ability and effort have to talk the talk to make up for their shortcomings. If you have found something really deep, especially that has the potential to help others, then it is really your duty to speak up and share.

Live everyday like you could die young

Steve Prefontaine died extremely young (aged twenty-four). There was of course a huge feeling that this was a waste of talent and it was so sad that we never got to see Steve Prefontaine in his prime years. This is no doubt true. Yet on a deeper level it encapsulated the Steve Prefontaine story even better because there was hardly more a man in history who lived everyday like it could be his last. The majority of people live so deeply in their comfort zone. In contrast Steve Prefontaine lived on the complete edge of his capabilities and pushed every ounce of his 'average talent' (in his own words) to the absolute maximum.

It is only in this space that we truly discover what it means to live. The vast majority of people are living like they are already dead (in state of comfort and fear of death) but I would implore you (using the spirit of Steve Prefontaine) as your guide to live life to the max. Risk it all. Be bold. Take courageous decisions. It is only by living like this that we truly learn what it means to be alive and also what it means to confront our death knowing that we actually lived. Then the fear of death starts to dissipate and even we die young, we know there is part of us that we touched through this extreme courage that will always live.

Articles 5: Relationships

How to overcome co-dependent relationships

Although I certainly had many flaws I was good at never ever ending up in co-dependent relationships. In fact I actually became very skilled at helping others who consistently ended up in them, as I worked on many different client cases around this issue.

Here I share three key points to help you end the co-dependency cycle.

Embrace your gifts and talents

Often co-dependency is a way to avoid fully embracing your gifts and talents. There is nothing like a co-dependent relationship to drain you of energy and to also stop you pursuing other things you could be doing that help you step into your full potential. Relationships should help you shine in all your glorious uniqueness. Often the best way to ensure this is to make investments in allowing you to explore this and be patient to allowing the 'right person' to show up at the right time. This person will encourage you to step into your fullest potential, where you are fully embracing your gifts and talents. They will not feel threatened or feel like they have to control you in anyway.

See relationships as an opportunity for growth rather than an end point

Many people approach relationships like it is an end point (i.e. being in a relationship is their highest ambition and once in a relationship all will be happy). This is a very destructive way to approach things. This is because fundamentally you are self-sabotaging yourself from reaching your full potential and also not facing the human reality of relationships. No relationship is ever going to be 'perfect'. All relationships will have conflicts, struggles and tense moments but these can really be profound and highly practical opportunities for growth if you allow them to be. When choosing a partner look for two things around this. Firstly look for someone who is prepared to grow and secondly look for someone who also wants to support your growth, without being controlling.

Learn to receive love not just give it

People in co-dependent relationships are often amazingly loving people, who always feel as though they are not giving enough love. This then easily gets taken advantage of. They love, love, love and the other person takes, takes, takes- neither is the good or bad person but both are dependent. One on being the unbalanced giver and the other on being the unbalanced taker. The solution is to learn to receive just as much love as you give others, so you can ensure balance and make the relationship co-thriving rather than co-dependent. You first need to learn to receive love off yourself. Behind this need to give, give, give lots of love is often deep levels of self-hatred and a very critical inner voice. By solving this you learn to receive more love off yourself. Over-time this then naturally translates into this being reflected outside of yourself, as you learn to receive more love off others too.

What to look for in an intimate relationship

We all love to make intimate relationships more complicated than they need to be. Especially when it comes to what we want. As spiritual people we often get caught up in either expecting far too much, creating grand concepts such as 'twin flames' or 'soul mates' that are only ever going to disappoint and over-analysing relationships to see how we are growing from them.

I propose simplicity, with a hefty dose of humanness to go along with it all too.

Firstly for a relationship to last in a vibrant way there often needs to be a strong sexual attraction. Forget compatibility, deep connection and spiritual synchronicity initially for now and instead focus on the very basic human need for sex. If a relationship is going to last in a healthy way you are going to have to want to fuck them regularly. Sometimes people seek other partners to satisfy this urge. Although there is nothing inherently wrong with that if your partner is happy with 'ethical polygamy' (what a ridiculous term by the way), I do always have strong feeling a great intimate relationship is based on 'unethical monogamy'. As in you don't have to pretend to be all ethical about it (hence unethical) but can at least honestly acknowledge that only fucking them is a cool way to create a deeper connection with another human being.

Secondly, along with sex, they have to meet your very other basic human needs that you want from an intimate relationship. These often vary a lot between people. And quite frankly most have no idea what they really want on a very basic human level, as it is easier to hide behind concepts and ideas that make it all sound so much more grand than it really is. How much money should they earn? What are they like emotionally? What are their aims in life? And many more questions that are really quite simple and dare I say dull. Often the best way to increase your chances of finding someone is to have lots of your needs met by family, friends and your career, so you are less restricted in exactly what you want from an intimate relationship. You are then free to allow more magic to come into your life.

Ok yes I admit it the final ingredient is often this intangible feeling or mysterious connection that can only be described as 'being in love'. I don't think we need to bring 'soul mates' and 'twin flames' into the love party, as it would be better to be able just to follow one's own intuition and big heart rather than need to match it up to some sort of ideal spiritual story. This is the missing ingredient that perhaps makes it the intimate relationship of your dreams and 'the one'. I do feel strongly, however, that without the basic human foundations provided from a strong sexual attraction and getting your other human needs met, then this mysterious thing called love can never really shine. This is why it is dangerous and immature just to pretend it is all about a 'spiritual connection' and a 'deeper connection' when the human reality never adds up to that unfortunately. This makes it no less mysterious though. If anything it becomes even more beautiful, as you balance the interaction between the very human part of you and the 'enlightened child' that will recognise the other when you meet them.

Articles 6: Healing
I healed a broken human being- so can you

The broken human being was of course me.

The PTSD from the random act of aggression in public was really the final tipping point in making me fully deal with my trauma. At the time it was hard to accurately put the story together but through much inner work and support from others I can share the below...

Something happened in childhood. I'm not exactly sure 100% what but it came up repeatedly in sessions with the different people I worked with and made perfect sense in the context of the overall picture of my life. It was deeply traumatic in nature. I was extremely disconnected from my body after this event, carrying a huge amount of emotional pain and had a feeling of having absolutely zero self-worth.

Recovery from all this wasn't fun at all- I had suffered deeply in my teenage years and University years because of this childhood trauma and lived a difficult life. The PTSD was a gift in many ways. It brought it all up right to the surface and gave me an opportunity to full deal with it all properly, without a sense of rush or having to achieve in other aspects of my life.

Here are 5 key lessons I would like to share about how to heal a broken human being. I have not only learnt this from my own healing journey but also supporting many clients through their own healing and trauma journey.

You need to deeply get into the body

The deepest layers of pain are really stored in the physical body. However, when a highly traumatic event takes place that is beyond the body's ability to deal with in the moment the trauma gets stored in an "energetic cloud". This "energetic cloud" is directly connected to part of the body that has completely shut down because of the trauma and will become re-activated slowly as you become strong enough in your body and spirit to deal with it.

What happens a lot in spiritual circles is that people use spirituality as a convenient way to escape their trauma and make it all sound very spiritual in the process. It breaks my heart actually. The person wants to connect to something that is more pure, peaceful and beautiful as described by whatever spiritual thing they are following but the reality is they can only do this if they are prepared to gently look at their trauma that is blocking a real re-connection with the spirit within. It is a painful process. And this is the reason why so many people quite frankly go around in circles for years on the spirtual path because it is just too painful to really look at the broken parts of themselves fully.

To avoid this get deeply into the body. Eat healthy, do exercise everyday (especially things such as yoga/Qi-Gong that promote more awareness), do massage, practice full awareness in intimacy and treat your body with the upmost love and care. Sometimes spiritual people are desperate to go beyond the body but I would always recommend deeply valuing your body no matter how spiritual you are.

The deepest emotions can only be let go in tenderness and vulnerability

As well as having a physical aspect, trauma creates a store of huge and powerful emotions to deal with. At the start it is tempting to run away and hide out in fake pseudo spiritual peace. Eventually we then realise we need to process the emotions to not only develop spiritually but quite frankly to be fully alive but there is again a trap. I see clients time and time again trying to force their emotions through a variety of methods. What needs to be seen is that the release of deep emotional pain is an incredibly feminine process, requiring tenderness, gentleness and an ability to really just let go. The deep emotion will come up at the right time. There is nothing to force, nothing to push and certainly nothing to process. It is just a deeper and deeper relaxation until you can finally come to a place of rest and let go with no effort.

Stay centred and patient

The secret to allowing trauma to unfold is to stay centred, with a healthy dose of patience. When the physical sensations, emotional pain and negative thoughts related to the trauma come up it is vital that you can feel them fully but also stay in a place of deep centredness. This is really the whole point of any spiritual development. The ability to be able to let the trauma play out on an inner level whilst also staying deeply centred in peace and your inner power is a deeply delicate and difficult process that takes many years to perfect. Patience is required. Trauma never

ever releases that quickly in my own personal experience and experience working with hundreds of clients. You need patience in not only developing your ability to stay centred but also worldly time patience in letting all the trauma work through your system. Does it ever fully release? I'm not convinced it does but what certainly can happen is you can be at complete peace with the releasing process to the point you are completely not traumatised anymore. A little bit of a paradox but very true.

Surround yourself with amazing people

We need human love. The worst thing about trauma is you get completely disconnected from human love and feel unlovable on a very deep level. You feel dirty, impure and disconnected. On my journey I walked alone for a long time. I was scared of the intimacy required to hold functional relationships, scared to be hurt again and most of all scared of the love revealing all the pain within. This was not sustainable. We all need to be surrounded by amazing grounded and normal worldly people who can give us much needed social interaction and the love that all the different parts of us need. It then becomes much easier to heal the trauma. It is not that these people help you directly heal the trauma but they offer a valuable support network that makes the overall process far easier.

Realise part of you can never be broken and everyone has very human parts (being fully healed is an illusion)

Functionality and a deep peace of mind are the name of the game. There will be people no doubt who have been traumatised far worse than I was and also those who really had nothing that would resemble trauma at all. All these people have one thing in common. No matter how much we have been broken or hurt there always remains part of ourselves that is unbroken and eternally pure- this is what a lot of the spirtual teachers/masters are trying to point towards and what we are all really seeking at a deeper level. It is important to try to connect with this on our spiritual path. It helps us realise that although fucking painful on a human level the truth is that the trauma is really just another story that makes up the existence of "me". It is very valid but on a certain level of reality is an illusion. This has to be balanced with the recognition that all human beings have a "me" that is made up of loads of conditioned behavioural patterns that enable us to be functional in different situations and environments. A lot of these patterns are quite fucked up but allowed us to survive certain childhood things. The key within all of this to tap into the deeper pure unchanging part regularly to get peace of mind, whilst also acknowledging that no matter how spiritual one is there are always going to be fucked up human parts that will never change.

The unity of all healing
Healing is actually very simple. What makes it complicated is human beings with their never-ending list of diseases and illnesses, all those "solutions" out there that imagine there is a power outside of yourself and a need to make my healing case special or unique.

If you want to heal here are three simple steps that will always work. I am not going to pretend these are easy- if they were the vast majority of people would be vibrantly healthy when anyone with two eyes can see that we don't live in a very healthy population in the Western World. These steps are simple but require discipline, commitment and often expert help.

The 3 simple steps to healing anything…

Treat the body with the upmost respect

This comes down to three key things- exercise, high quality diet and adequate sleep/rest. Exercise should be something that helps get you fitter, moving and is enjoyable to do. Ideally it also promotes higher levels of body awareness and energises the subtle energy system (think things such as yoga, Tai Chi or Qi-Gong). The specifics of a high quality diet are unique to you but would encompass lots of fruit and veg, drinking lots of water, no alcohol, a good balance of grains/meat as desired and maybe a high-quality vitamin/mineral supplement. Food you eat should feel simple, easy and enjoyable. Finally so many people are way too over-busy. Healing requires a huge amount of energy, so you need to ensure you are doing your best to encourage adequate sleep/rest in your life. An afternoon nap can never be over-rated nor the ability to only have to get up in the morning when your body wakes up (no alarms).

Releasing emotional pain

Most things that need to be healed are really underpinned by a huge amount of unseen emotional pain. This is very difficult to full grasp until you have been through it. The best example of this in my opinion is chronic fatigue, which I overcame and have helped others heal- there is no known real medical cure for this and I would suggest it is really the result of the body using a phenomenal amount of energy stopping you feeling the full brunt of severe emotional pain. Process the emotion and the chronic fatigue goes. For other things I would say it is less simple but the principle still holds that one needs to release a huge amount of emotional pain in nearly any healing case.

But how to do this?

There are three key points. The first bit of good news is that if you took the first principle of treating your body with the upmost respect seriously, then you have already conquered key point number one. Emotions only heal through the body-emotional field; you simply can't process them unless you are properly or at least partially in your body. I can't over-emphasise this point enough- get in the body, get in the body, get in the body. If there was one point I would share with spiritual people looking to heal it would be this, as so many are using spirituality to escape their body and real healing, whilst making it all seem very spiritual and noble in the process. The second key point is really allowing yourself to feel all the range of emotions we carry without shame or guilt. In the Western World we are trained to be very supressed. It is important to give yourself space during the day (whether in meditation, a walk in nature or talking to a trusted person) to really feel what is happening inside of you and doing your best to allow it all to come up. It is amazing what we can carry inside of us. Finally emotions (especially those that are held deeply in the system from trauma) take so long to fully free up and start to really process, so a hefty dose of patience is encouraged. The deepest emotions are felt in the deepest vulnerability. It is not a pushing and masculine action that is needed to release the deepest emotions but a tender, vulnerable and feminine non-action with patience at it's core.

Learn to re-connect to the enlightened child within

No matter how much you need to heal on a human level there is a place within us all that is already fully healed. I call this place "the enlightened child". It is pure, innocent, incorruptible, whole, healed, eternally peaceful and whatever spiritual words you want to associate with it. It is what all the spiritual masters/gurus/teachers are pointing towards in their own unique way.

It is critical for healing.

It completely changes the dynamic of everything because you find this place inside of you that can never be broken and will remain untouched no matter the pain you may be going through on a human level. Does it speed up the healing process? I think it is actually dis-connected to the healing process of the body and other things that may appear to need to be healed in the world bar in the fact that it makes it all much easier to witness from a place of wonder and peace.

There are no miracles in the world apart from the person who can go through their deepest human pain, whilst also staying connected in some part to the "enlightened child" within. So do both. Connect to the "enlightened child" through whatever spiritual means you want too and most of all get deeply into the body and your emotions if you want to process what is holding you back from healing on a human level.

Final thoughts

All healing is really the same on a human level- get into the body and process the emotions. Of course there are many individual specifics along this journey. I would never draw anyone away from traditional medicine and using common sense but at the same time would always emphasising getting into the body deeply and processing emotions as the key. Then I would share a point of healing not in this world and known by very few...the "enlightened child" within. The point of going beyond it all, not to some magical place outside of yourself and own power but simply a re-connection to what has always been there and always will be.

148

Articles 7: Diet
3 lessons on diet from a raw vegan meat eater

I have gone under many identities over the years. Sometimes Jack, sometimes Jay-Jay and sometimes a certain diet. At various times in my life I have introduced myself as a "raw vegan", "fruitarian", "vegan" and "vegetarian" depending on what exact diet I was eating at the time.

Me and diet go way back.

It all started when I was in my teenage years with severe digestive issues and diet became the answer to my terrible health and pain. Firstly I stayed conventional. I tried to eat a more healthy version of a normal standard Western diet but when that didn't work I had to transition to a vegetarian diet, then a vegan diet, then a raw vegan diet and eventually a pure fruitarian diet.

Mangos for breakfast, bananas for lunch and nectarines for dinner.

No-one could accuse me of not getting enough sugar or enough fruit in my diet. Perhaps there were other accusations people could and did throw at me about the limitations of my diet but before the nutritionally aware amongst you have a Quinoa attack I would like to share I was physically thrivingly healthy as a fruitarian and even ran a 31 mile ultramarathon when on the diet. Not bad going to be fair.

Anyway all this experimentation- going from Standard Western all the way to fruitarian and ultimately back again gave me a huge amount of insight. Here I share 3 lessons on diet from a raw vegan meat eater...

Different diets worked for me at different points in my life- I firmly believe there is no "best diet". Every diet has its perks. When I was healing from severe digestive issues a really pure raw vegan diet worked wonders for me but once I had significantly healed the trauma underlying this then I could enjoy the freedom of eating normally again. Because lets face it- raw vegan wasn't the best thing socially! Everyone in the diet world seriously needs to relax. A lot of people who eat standard Western hate the vegetarians/vegans (in all fairness the preachy ones are bloody annoying), the vegetarians hate the vegans, the vegans hate the raw vegans, the raw vegans hate the fruitarians and I'm not exactly sure who the fruitarians hate? Maybe the breatharians? Those guys are a whole other breed entirely. Anyway the point is lots of people within a certain diet community want to believe their diet is the best diet because it re-enforces their belief system about nutrition, themselves and aspects of life. A real spiritual person would see all this is false and quite frankly a person should be free to eat exactly what they want without judgement.

There is nothing more spiritually pure about not eating animals- sorry to burst the spiritual bubble and reveal myself as an unethical meat-eater spiritual fraud but I have a confession to make. I really like cheese, chicken and steak. Some people seem to believe that eating a certain way makes them more spiritually pure or even above others but my own self-enquiry has shown me I can feel happy, "pure" and good about myself spiritually no matter what I am eating. Even the double cheese burger and Mcflurry from Mcdonalds tastes good with this attitude.

Strict and rigid diets often hide trauma and emotional pain- those who take diet very seriously, with rigidness and strictness, are often hiding a lot of trauma and emotional pain. I certainly was. It takes immense bravery to change your diet in search of something better but it takes even more bravery to let go of something that has worked for you in search of a deeper truth. My change in diet to raw vegan made a huge positive difference to my life on many levels but I saw very clearly how it had become a massive block on my spiritual journey because I was reliant on it to feel healthy, happy and good about myself. THIS IS NOT FREEDOM PEOPLE!

5 important points on diet to help bring peace of mind

Having been through the whole spectrum of diets (standard Western, vegetarian, vegan, raw vegan, fruitarian and then back to standard Western again) I feel I have a deep understanding on the topic. Especially on how to truly heal and develop spiritually through diet. Here are 5 important points on diet to help you get peace of mind...

Eat simply

The body loves simplicity. Eating simply helps you have more energy, as much physical energy is lost in the digestive process which eating simply improves. The mind also love simplicity. Simple meals mean you don't have to put much mental energy into your meals, which helps free up space to use it on far more important aspects of life.

Eat from a place of love

The vast majority of people on "diets" are really eating from a place of fear and self-hatred. This is often what causes all the digestive issues on a deeper level, as well as many other problems associated with diet. Eating food should be an enjoyable, slow and maybe even sensual process. There is nothing enjoyable and certainly nothing sensual about counting calories/fat/protein, worrying about vitamins/minerals or stressing over whether you are eating healthily enough. Before eating, breath and really take time to slow down. So often in life we are rushed and busy but when we eat we should really give ourselves the gift of slowing down and eating from a place of love.

Eat chocolate cake for breakfast

Ok maybe not literally but the deeper point is that sometimes it is best to throw all discipline and structure out of the window to really enjoy a naughty treat in all it's glory. The main thing that will cause problems from food is eating from guilt. So experiment and do some crazy things to test how easily your mind goes into guilt over diet and how stressed you actually are over the whole eating diet process.

Eat flexibly

Try your best not to attach yourself to meaningless labels such as "vegetarian", "vegan", "raw vegan" "X diet" etc. You are a human being enjoying the food that feels best for you at this moment in time. Nothing more complicated than that.

Eat lots of human love

Unfortunately they don't sell human love in the food aisles because if they did it would be the most sweet, beautiful, satiating and in demand food treat in the world. The main reason we over-eat or get obsessed over diet is because we lack human love. Human love for ourselves and human love from others. So think outside of the very limited diet box and really try to feel into what it is you truly want behind your need to focus on diet. You may be surprised by the results.

<u>3 steps to consider before you start an enlightened online business</u>

Wowza, starting a business can appear complicated when you look into it. A couple of years ago I started to look into how best I could start an online business and was over-whelmed with how much conflicting advice there was out there. So many different approaches and angles to consider. Should I focus on social media? Should I give away free sessions to entice clients? Should I do individual sessions or build a programme? Should I create a funnel? Did I need a blog and a website?

I want to simplify things for those of you who want to come at starting an online business from an enlightened perspective.

There are three very key steps that I would share below...

Be very clear on what you want

This sounds obvious but it really isn't. So many approaches and 'business gurus' out there are working on the underlying assumption that you are exactly like them and also that success is how big you can grow your business. This is so fundamentally flawed and causes people so much pain. We are all designed to manifest and live our highest potential in such different ways, which means that how we set-up our business needs to reflect this rather than just copying someone else's technique. Often the best thing to do is go with what you enjoy. For example I really enjoy writing and it comes very naturally to me, so I put a big focus on writing books and guest blogs that get my name out there. I don't enjoy being on social media. In the future I may go down the social media avenue as I enjoy creating content but I would only do it when I could employ someone who could look after it all for me, so I could focus solely on the content. It is the same with marketing. I am happy to produce content but since I don't enjoy the whole marketing and sales process, I try to delegate this as best I can. Secondly success is much more than how big your business grows. I have met many people who seem to be 'thriving' with their business when you just look from the outside but tear away the veil and all is not as happy as it seems. They have zero time freedom, their relationships are suffering and they are so stressed out from their business that all joy has gone from their life. So be very clear what you want from your business and how it fits into the bigger picture of our lives. Surely the best question to ask is how can I help others as much as possible and create a life of joy? From that simple but highly powerful and effective question, the answer to how your business fits into your life should hopefully flow. If it doesn't then keep going back to it regularly as you take action and over-time it will become more and more clear.

Focus on getting paid clients

You don't really have a business until you are working with a client. So many people get stuck in the trap of creating excuses as to why they need to do X before they can start working with paid clients. They are all really blocks. Things like I need to build my website, I need to build my social media, I need to do some practice free sessions and I need to build my brand are all just garbage designed to block you from the fear of working with a paid client for the first time. Focus relentlessly on getting paid clients. If you do this, obvious and simple solutions should emerge rather than 'fake solutions' that waste a lot of your time and block the time you could be working with paid clients.

Take action

This is similar to the point above but makes other aspects of it even more clear. The successful people are the ones who take action aligned to a goal they are working towards- they are not over-planning, they are not thinking about it, they are not doing it in six months time, they are doing it now. Take action, take action, take action. Even if you don't get quite what you want immediately from taking action, you learn valuable information and things about yourself that help you get there much quicker in the long-run.

Recovering From Career Setbacks

It was fair to say I have had my fair share of career setbacks. It is the nature of High Performance Sport unfortunately, particularly as a young coach with ambition and talent.

Here I share my 5 top tips for navigating a career setback where you lose your job- they are particularly likely on a spiritual enlightenment path, as the universe seeks to wake up you a little or send you in a new direction.

Slow down

There is no need to jump straight back into work after a career setback bar of course unless you really really have to for financial reasons. I find this is rare amongst spiritual seekers. If the universe really wants you to take some time out, you can be sure you will be covered financially and your needs will be met. Often why people want to jump straight back in has nothing to do with money. Instead money is often the veil for wanting to avoid the emotional pain, the void of not knowing and the loss of worldly status that seems to come with a career setback. It is best to put these things aside. It is only by slowing down that we can truly start to integrate the pain and lessons of what has taking place, allowing us to grow in optimal ways.

Learn some new skills

People are so busy these days. Often all we are really doing is surviving and repeating the same thing over and over, without really developing ourselves on a practical human level or a deeper spiritual level. A career setback is an opportunity to learn some new practical skills. Perhaps the painting you always wanted to do, the book you always wanted to write, the holistic therapy you always wanted to train in or the progression to your education you never made. If a career setback isn't the time to do these things there probably will never be a time.

Go deeper on your enlightenment path

Being busy constantly (avoiding emotions) or being resistance to participating in the world in the name of 'spirituality' are both extremes we should look to avoid. A career setback offers the perfect opportunity to find balance. Often because of the nature of modern life we are generally going to have to be more busy than is perhaps optimal for most people's spiritual growth, so a career setback enables us to re-balance and spend some much needed time on putting number enlightenment first. You can meditate for hours each day, spend some proper quality time integrating any healing work you do and really start to question what would be a great next step for you, without the hussle and bussle of normal life getting in your way.

Consider- do I need to go back into that career world?

It is extremely difficult to accurately say whether when you lose a job (often through circumstances not really in your control the more advanced you get), you should go back into the same career field or not. Generally you should. Often what spiritual people and I certainly did (after the PTSD trauma from the loss of one job) is to run away as far as possible from the same career field to avoid the pain. This is not good for your enlightenment path. Sometimes, especially when you are older and have been in a career field for a considerable amount of time (as well as being very well sorted financially), the universe is telling you 'come on mate move on!'. This is rare though. I would generally question if someone wants to radically change career path-evolve yes and maybe go into a different aspect of it but extreme changes usually hint at an avoidance of pain (spiritual escapism).

Make connections

When we lose a job, especially one we love, it often makes us feel isolated and perhaps that even the whole world is against us. We need a different mindset for optimal success. The increased time you have can be used to make connections (not just career ones) that you have left redundant because of how busy you have been with a previous job. Often surprises are in store when we make connections. Speaking to others often results in the universe putting messages through other people (little hints that help you on your way if you are aware) and can even sometimes result in 'miracles' occurring that offer you a direct connection to your next step. If you don't put yourself out there though you can be certain nothing will happen.

Finding a suitable career

The beauty of connecting to the 'enlightened child' within is that you can accept your humanity fully. This takes a lot of pressure off. The pressure to pretend to be spiritual, the pressure to earn status and pride from how much you earn in the world and the pressure to have to make your career look a certain way so you can come across more spiritual and enlightened to the outside world. It allows some honesty.

Although the 'enlightened child' only comes in one shapeless and formless dimension, human beings come in all shapes and forms. This includes their career. We all have such varied natural gifts and talents, life circumstances that affect our career decisions and things that we want to achieve. This means that how one 'enlightened career' may look for one person is very different to an 'enlightened career' for another person. And the 'enlightened child' couldn't' care less. Its only directionless motive is to use your humanity to its fullest potential to inspire and point others towards their own 'enlightened child'. It is that simple.

I believe finding a suitable career is an extremely important thing to talk about for someone interested in enlightenment. For most of us it is a massive human dilemma, as the vast majority of our time is going to be spent on it and it is going to be the main way we learn about and share the 'enlightened child'. An incredibly worthwhile discussion to be had. With this in mind I want to share some simple yet profound things to consider when finding a suitable career for you…

Start from the basics

It is best not to be too grand about things initially and start from the basics of what you want from your career. Key things include how much money you want to earn, how it fits in with other key commitments (such as children, relationships etc) and whether it looks like a relatively sustainable career in the modern world. These boxes need to be ticked before one can dream. If something really is meant to happen or is in 'your highest good' then you can be sure that these basic needs will also be met.

Focus on what brings you joy

If you are going to have to spend a huge amount on your career (as we nearly all have to do), then it makes a lot of sense to focus on having a career that brings you a lot of joy. This will vary a lot person to person. The key is really actually knowing yourself on a deeper enough level to separate what you actually want in your heart from what you have been conditioned to want in a way that disconnects you from your heart. The process can be simple or complex. What this really reflects is how simply or complexly you are disconnected from your heart, which is then reflected back to you in your career. Joy is in the heart.

Let purpose unfold with no need for a higher purpose

Purpose will unfold in its own accord. Many people seek to end their constant dissatisfaction (which really all stems from a disconnection to the 'enlightened child') by searching for a higher purpose in their career. I would caution against this. It often leads to ungrounded decisions being made, trying to seek purpose in the world rather than the human heart and disconnects you strongly from the purposelessness of the 'enlightened child' if you believe your own higher purpose too strongly. Have no purpose and be free.

Articles 9: Enlightenment

The Human Condition

I firmly believe we should have a lot more compassion for our human condition. In many ways we are all like lost children, trying to make sense of the world and do the best we can with our lives.

Below is what I have discovered about the human condition- in many ways it is very simple but is vital to understand on the spiritual path because no matter how much you develop you will always remain human!

From my own humble self-inquiry I believe we all carry what I term an "enlightened child" within and then have bodily sensations, emotions, thoughts and energetic sensations all wrapped within conditioned specific patterns of behaviour that help us live in the world.

The "enlightened child"

This is what all the great spiritual masters/gurus/teachers have been pointing towards throughout time. I just call it the "enlightened child" because I feel like it. "Enlightened" helps demonstrate it is full of light and is something not of this world, whilst "child" points towards the fact it is in every human being and is very pure/ incorruptible like a child (bar those few little bastards we all come across now and again!).

The most important point that beyond all the spirtual terms/concepts/ideas/traditions the real purpose of a spiritual path is to re-connect with the "enlightened child" essence within us. Everything outside of this is to fulfil your human needs.

The human being

The perceptive in the spiritual world soon discover that a lot of spirituality is really done by people looking to fulfil their human needs- a sense of love, a sense of community and often a sense of specialness wrapped up in pretend spiritual "non-specialness". There is of course nothing wrong with this. Yet to confuse it with "real spirituality" (i.e. the search for the enlightened child) would be to do yourself a disservice and also make your spiritual behaviour appear a lot more unhuman that it actually truly is.

Personally I have a massive passion for spirituality and enlightenment but also prefer to explore that part of my life within the recognition that I would prefer to live a relatively normal life in the world- surrounded by lots of family/friends with different interests to me, doing sports coaching work I love outside of the spiritual work and just enjoying all the pleasures of Earth (food, sex, television etc).

An outstanding discovery I made on my spiritual path was that we will always retain our conditioned patterns of behaviour- the difference as we mature on the spiritual path isn't that these suddenly disappear and we become unconditioned but is we become more aware of what best conditioned behavioural pattern to choose in a certain situation.

I can't emphasise this point enough- the human being will always remain! The vast majority of spiritual gurus/masters/teachers are almost pretending that the human being doesn't exist but surely there are only two real purposes to spirtuality? Firstly to re-connect to the "enlightened child" on a deeper and deeper level and secondly to use your greater awareness to make sure you enjoy life as much as possible. You know for career success, loving relationships and vibrant health. Sorry to burst the grandeur of the spiritual bubble but I honestly believe it is as simple as that.

The search for spiritual enlightenment- confessions of a human being

"Spiritual enlightenment" has to be the most over-rated and misunderstood concept in the history of humanity. Here I share some confessions as a human being as to what I found from an intensive search over a number of years

After the unexpected breakdown of my life I was a man on a mission. Firstly the mission was to heal the PTSD so I could actually function in the world again but on a deeper level the search was for a place beyond all pain and suffering. "Spiritual enlightenment" was the goal.

Over the preceding years I worked with many spiritual teachers/masters, trained in a wide range of modalities and spent hundreds of hours in meditation in search of the holy grail. Here are some of the shocking things I found about "spiritual enlightenment"...

1. Everyone will always be human- there will always be emotions, thoughts, bodily sensations, energetic sensations and maybe even some sort of "spiritual experiences". This is called being human and doesn't change no matter how enlightened you become.

2. **There is no authority on enlightenment-** spiritual teachers/masters often point the wrong way. It is better to use your common sense and get help when needed but fundamentally you must walk alone with loving friends/family in normal life.

3. **It is much better to stay in the world-** the world is far more fun than living in isolation and often much richer in learning too, since relationships are the main things that trigger us.

4. **There does appear to be something but I wouldn't call it enlightenment-** it is re-connection to peace

5. **Personality has nothing to do with enlightenment-** no single personality is more enlightened than any other. Stop playing games and accept your full humanity

6. **The enlightened can have sex-** the whole of the spiritual world (bar maybe the tantric world) seems obsessed with avoiding that sex exists in the human world. The enlightened are allowed to have sex.

7. **The enlightened can have fun-** holy shamoly the spiritual world is full of boring people, particularly the teachers/masters. You would have thought their spiritual insights would have livened them up a little. The enlightened are allowed to have fun, ideally a huge amount of it.

8. **The enlightened can have opinions and judgements-** it is quite difficult to function in the modern world without them to be honest. This one is all about level confusion. One can appear to have an opinion and judgement and opinion on something in the world, whilst at a deeper level coming from a place of non-judgement

9. **The most enlightened often aren't spiritual teachers-** they instead just enlighten people through their everyday work in normal life

10. **You are much closer to enlightenment at the start of your spiritual journey-** the search often takes you away from enlightenment.

The interesting thing about enlightenment is how it interacts with your humanity

Enlightenment only becomes interesting when you examine how it interacts with your humanity. If you were to listen to the vast number of spiritual gurus/masters/teachers, you would imagine that enlightenment is the end goal in itself and this mystical magical thing that will be revealed only after an extensive purification and disciplined process. It is also this thing that has nothing to do with your humanity. It is as if almost the human being becomes irrelevant when the talk turns to enlightenment and only grand spiritual concepts far beyond the realms of a normal human experience are worth mentioning.

What utter garbage and what a grand deception.

As someone who has been enlightened since the age of twenty I can tell you with full honesty that the most interesting thing is how it interacts with your humanity- namely the body, the emotions, the thoughts and the subtle energies. Or even more specifically how it interacts with the conditioned 'me' (that absolutely never goes away by the way) to produce an enlightened yet functional human being who can operate with success in the world. With vibrant health, loving relationships and career achievement, whilst also retaining the connection to the peace, innocence and nothingness everythingness of the 'enlightened child' within.

Now that is truly interesting.

How can one live in this competitive dog eat cat modern world whilst also staying connected to the 'enlightened child' that doesn't in recognise the world as existing? How can one enjoying fucking the living daylights out of another human being with maximum pleasure whilst also staying connected to the 'enlightened child' that wants to use your sexual energy for transformation? How can one find peace and balance in all types of worldly relationships whilst also staying connected to the 'enlightened child' that can only ever be found in total aloneness?

I don't propose an answer to any of these questions. What I do propose though is a normal radical realisation that this is where the real enlightenment and real life is- in the exploration (not answer; there is no answer) of the interaction of the 'enlightened child' with the human being. All teachers trying to just teach about enlightenment/'the enlightened child' are at best

161

doing you a disservice and at worst keeping you and them in total ignorance, as they are missing the fundamental point that the enlightenment can only ever be realised on the Earth through the ordinary function of a human being. There is no other way.

Printed in Great Britain
by Amazon